Advance Praise for
The Mind of a Millionairess

"Jewel is a mogul, a mentor, a lifter of women, and a manager of wealth. Thank you for elevating my thought process as it relates to money, investment, and building a financial legacy. I love and celebrate you!"

—**Holly Carter**, Hollywood producer

"Jewel has a way of making you want to learn all this stuff! I'd heard about cryptocurrency and didn't understand it until she started breaking it down to where I could appreciate it! She was super patient and walked me through accumulating crypto! Now I'm a real holder (buying and holding); I'm too excited about becoming a crypto millionaire!"

—**DeeDee Freeman**

"Jewel has an ability to make you wanna learn and build wealth for yourself and not wait for anyone else! For me her teaching reinforced what I was thinking! Reading the book puts you on the right path for building wealth with all these new rules!"

—**Dr. Heavenly Kimes**

THE MIND OF A

Millionairess

JEWEL TANKARD

Post Hill
PRESS

A POST HILL PRESS BOOK

The Mind of a Millionairess
© 2021 by Jewel Tankard
All Rights Reserved

ISBN: 978-1-63758-032-5
ISBN (eBook): 978-1-63758-033-2

Cover art by Dorian Kirkwood
Interior design and composition by Greg Johnson, Textbook Perfect

Post Hill Press
New York • Nashville
posthillpress.com

Published in the United States of America
1 2 3 4 5 6 7 8 9 10

To my mom and my grandmothers
for being powerful women.
I've profited from your strength
and learned from your lives the importance
of trusting my financial instinct.

Contents

Foreword

by Kim Kiyosaki

The rules around money and women have changed dramatically.

As women growing up, not only were we not expected to know much about money, we were actually taught to depend upon someone else for our financial well-being: a husband, a family member, or the government. And today, statistics prove again and again that due to divorce, death of a spouse, or poor money skills, women are finding themselves in a financial crisis.

This is why today, more than ever, it is so important for women to become financially savvy. To become not only financially secure but financially independent. Why? Because money has the power to enslave us, and it has the power to set us free. I am all about women being free. Free to go for your dreams. Free to live the life *you* choose.

For years I have been an advocate for women to rise up and become the financial pillars in their families, communities, and beyond. I will admit, it is not an easy path. But it is the most rewarding if you choose to take it.

In today's world of uncertainty and volatile changes, the question to ask yourself is, "What can I control?" The answer is YOU. You can control you. You cannot control what the government will do. You cannot control what Wall Street is going to do. But you can control what you do.

This is where Jewel and her brilliance of *Mind of a Millionairess* shines through. Jewel is a true role model for women, not only in the world of money and investing, but even more importantly in her ability to create and help others create the mindset necessary for financial success. She never lets the setbacks and obstacles stop her. She has the courage to break free of her comfort zone and to go well beyond what she knows. She never quits when the going gets tough, and most importantly she has never quit on herself and her dreams. Jewel is a *real* teacher. By that I mean she practices what she preaches. If she is teaching it, then she has done it. And that is why I am very honored to call Jewel my friend.

It is one thing to say, "Yes, I want to be wealthy. I want to be financially free." It's another to do what truly needs to be done to get there. Jewel and her Millionairess mindset is the perfect guide for your journey. A great teacher doesn't give you the answers, she inspires you to learn and to go for your dreams. The Millionairess mindset is one of transformation. Who you will become in this process will amaze and excite you. Your confidence, courage, clarity, and knowledge will soar.

If you truly want to transform your life then I encourage you to take the Millionairess journey with Jewel. This adventure is for women who want much more in life, who are not afraid to take on new challenges, and most importantly who are willing to stand up and be role models for women throughout the world. This is your time.

"There is no force equal to a woman determined to rise."
—W.E.B. Du Bois

Introduction

Yes, Girl!
You *Can* Have It All!

Hey, girl! I am so excited that you are here with me to invest in your future and financial well-being. You deserve this investment in yourself. So many times we will invest in every other area our lives—we learn how to cook, how to eat healthy, and all kinds of things—but we don't take the time we need to invest in what will allow us to live at a level of freedom that sometimes only financial wealth can afford. You know, money affects how we move in the world—where we live, what we drive, what tables we are invited to, what power we have to influence our community and world, and what access we have to certain people and opportunities. I don't know about you, but I don't want anything cramping my lavish style.

Financial tools and wealth-creation strategies are constantly changing, and even if you have attended a financial workshop or read a book or two before, you need the most current information to build and continue to build wealth today. The methods your grandparents—or even your parents—may have used to manage their finances or build wealth are antiquated and will not bring you into your wealthy place today. But don't worry, girl. I got you! I am here as your personal wealth strategist, and will help to release your potential for achieving high levels of success in your personal and financial life.

Whether you're an entrepreneur, a business executive, or a corporate or blue-collar worker, you deserve to live your dreams. Deep down inside, you know this. You desire to have more than enough. You are that girl who is hungry and wants more out of life. You are that girl who always looks to go above and beyond.

Maybe you love the finer things in life—red bottoms, a Gucci bag, Chanel shades, an exclusive tropical vacay, a beautiful home, and a brand-new foreign car. But what's recently been plaguing you is what's left—or what *isn't* left—at the end of the month, and Christian Louboutin isn't paying the rent or your light bill. What opportunities do you have that pay you, line your bank accounts, and set up a financial future for your kids and kids' kids?

Or maybe you aren't a spendthrift—but the way you learned to budget your money and live below your means isn't paying off the way the experts said it would. And how could it, if their main goal is to help you get out of debt and live on a small budget, but not to teach you how to increase your earnings and build wealth? Living on a shoestring budget may be okay for some, but not for you, my millionairess-in-the-making. That millionairess lifestyle is calling out to you, and I have the cutting-edge information and inside track to new money tools and resources that will help you answer the call to living your most amazing life.

Packed within the pages of this book are paradigm-shifting, mindset-altering insights and revelations about money, wealth building, and creating a financial legacy that will give you the motivation you need to discover and develop the millionairess in you. In every chapter, you will be met with new and challenging concepts that may seem difficult or intimidating at first, but that's okay. You are up for the challenge, right?

I'm an economist turned financial powerhouse, and I'm taking the world by storm. As a serial network marketer, I've grossed over $5 million and empowered over 250,000 people in my robust organizations. I've created a global reputation for creating multiple 6–7 figure earners with my success strategies. I will make sure that what I teach will be easy for you to grasp and implement immediately. Features like Jewel's Gems, Jewel's Jumpstarts, charts, tables, and graphs will highlight powerful nuggets and transformative actions steps that will help you build a solid foundation toward creating a financial dynasty beyond what you ever thought possible. Here's your first one:

Jewel's Gem

The difference between the rich and poor is information.

Like any good coach or mentor, I am going to help you confront some things about yourself that need to change in order to see transformation in your life. Don't be afraid. *Be excited.* Be open and ready to receive new ideas. Change doesn't always feel good. Sometimes it is painful, but just by picking up this book, I believe you are ready to move from your comfort zone into what I call the "trust zone." I believe you are ready for your pain to have purpose. Rather than allowing pain to keep you from achieving your goals, you can harness its power to push you into that metamorphic process—ultimately turning you into the woman you dream of becoming.

Wealth creation is intentional. It takes vision, focus, discipline, and consistent activity. This book will help you know what those activities are by unlocking the keys to wealth and helping you find your own path to creating it for yourself. Use this book as your blueprint for success. Read each chapter carefully and complete the suggested action steps. Pay attention, take plenty of notes, write down the ideas that come to you as you read, and most importantly, act quickly. Don't spend all this time learning only to do nothing. It's always better to do something than nothing at all.

Jewel's Gem

It's better to do something than nothing at all!

By the end of this book you should be thinking and looking differently, while growing your investments and your brand, your money, and your financial legacy.

The Millionairess Mind

According to the 2019 Market Insight Report by Spectrem, only 3 percent of households in the United States have a net worth of more than $1 million. One reason why wealth isn't held by more households is because wealth requires embracing an entirely different thinking pattern, and many people are not ready to make the changes that allow for this thinking pattern to take root and manifest in their lives. Anytime you prepare to go to a new level in your personal or financial growth, understand that not everyone will see the same vision you see for yourself or comprehend the new concepts you are adopting. You will often leave the majority behind. People who are not open to making the necessary changes are generally not afraid of success; rather, they are afraid of failure, afraid that success will not happen. Fear stops them in their tracks.

To acquire and maintain the mind of a millionairess, the old mind must be renewed, which is exactly why your mindset, behaviors, and beliefs about money will be the first area we will address in this journey. You must have the mindset for the discipline, patience, perseverance, and risk tolerance it takes to create wealth. Then you must also know that you can trust your financial gut.

How I Learned to Trust My Gut and Earn My First Million

I am a fourth-generation entrepreneur. My parents, Earthel and June LaGreen, were the first African Americans to own a business in downtown Detroit. They made a very good living as the owners of LaGreen's Records and Tapes. They had three locations in downtown Detroit, and I watched as they interacted with their customers. All the popular Motown artists frequented their record stores. I remember seeing stars like Peabo Bryson, Minnie Riperton, Phyllis Hyman, and so many more. LaGreen's Records and Tapes was a premier place for artists to sign CDs, host listening parties, and connect with their listeners.

Mom and Dad were a power couple before people started using that term. They lived a fabulous lifestyle with his and her Mercedes-Benzes, his and her Rolls-Royces, housekeepers, cooks, and drivers.

Growing up in Detroit was a pretty amazing experience. I had a great childhood, and went to the best private schools. I lived in a great neighborhood and had a Volvo as my first car at the age of sixteen.

And then, when I was nineteen, we lost everything.

I was devastated. I couldn't figure out how we had gone from having everything to having nothing. I asked my mother question after question, trying to understand what had happened: "Do we have money saved? Do we have anything paid off or any investments?"

Her answers were always, "You know, your father thought this," "Your father saw that," "Your father wanted to do this," or, "Your father didn't want to do that."

It became clear to me that my mom really didn't trust her gut—her own financial instinct—to give input and make decisions regarding our family's money issues.

For a while, this made me angry with her. I felt that if she had done her part and made some investments like she wanted to and also saved some money, she could have saved the day like Angela Bassett's character, Mrs. Watson, did in the movie *Jumping the Broom*. In the movie, Mrs. Watson's husband was losing everything, but because his wife had made some wise investments, their lifestyle wasn't interrupted. Now, I know that was a movie, but at nineteen years old, the concept that women should trust their financial gut and can be the financial heroes seemed like the ideal solution to me.

Pain Pushed Me into My Purpose

After my family's financial loss, I started dating Detroit drug dealers. It was somewhat of a glamorous lifestyle. Every girl wanted a dope boy, so that's what I went after too. It was fun for a while...until they began to get indicted and sent to jail. Or they died. I went to church thinking I was going to pray this one particular drug kingpin out of jail. *Yes, girl*, that was me.

Eventually, I got married but not to the right guy. But who could tell me that at the time? I thought I knew it all. Within two years, my marriage, which had become abusive, was over. I was left alone with a beautiful baby girl and a broken heart.

The divorce was crazy, and I had fallen on hard times. I was on food stamps for almost a year, trying to figure it out and make sure my daughter was taken care of. Then one day, I just sort of had this epiphany. I declared to myself, "I am not about to be that girl who's waiting on child support to determine whether or not her daughter can go to private school or if I can drive the car of my dreams."

This surge of strength and belief just rose up in me: that I deserved more, that I was not a child-support-living kind of girl. (Even though I *was* looking for that check to come in at the time. Let me just be real, okay?) I did not want to move through life like that. I was determined that that would not be my narrative. That would not be my story.

I was a student at the University of Michigan, majoring in economics. My goal was to understand patterns and rhythms of money. I was also working as an actress and model. But my belief that I deserved more led me to begin asking myself some serious questions like, "Why can't you take care of yourself?"

Through the self-questioning, I discovered I had a strong desire to own my own business—a desire I'm sure came from watching my parents run their own business. So, I jumped on an opportunity to partner with a gentleman who owned a chain of soul food restaurants. He and I opened a Nextel franchise. It was very successful and grew from nothing into a staff of about fifteen the first year. After acquiring large contracts with companies like Mishcon de Reya, I made my first million dollars.

Busy in my new life and business, I had a sweet interruption and met the man of my dreams (and prayers): Pastor Ben Tankard, my honey and lifetime groom. Twenty years later, we are a beautiful, blended family with five children—Marcus, Brooklyn, Britney, Benji, and Cyrene—all grown, out of college, and living their lives. We co-pastor Destiny Center Church in Murfreesboro, Tennessee, and operate several thriving businesses.

How All This Led Me to You

While experiencing phenomenal success in my first business, I noticed that across the board, not many women were working in the financial industry. We were not dominating in real estate, oil, or precious metals. To remedy this and help women get educated in these wealth-building opportunities, ones I had come to profit from, I decided to create a community. I aimed to provide a safe place for women who, like me, wanted to be wildly successful. This community, which I call "The Millionairess Club," is where we learn ways to have success in our personal, professional, and family lives. The Millionairess Club is committed to helping women of color create wealth. The club empowers the women to trust their financial gut, improves their confidence, gives them cash creation and wealth growing strategies, and introduces them to modern investment tools.

As a Christian, moving in the world with faith as my center is critical. It forms the basis for why it is important to me to create wealth opportunities for myself, my family, and amazing women like you. God was clear that He came so that we would have life and have life more abundantly—but at some point, it got twisted to where people think that if you want to have a relationship with Jesus, you have to be broke or modest with material things. But

God is extravagant, and I am God's girl, so you know…I have to represent Him well.

I have been blessed to learn and be exposed to many opportunities that the average girl may not think are available for her. But I am here to tell you, girl, you can get in the game and play in the financial fields too. And you don't have to be a millionaire to do it. You just have to have a growth mindset.

What I have for you in the pages of this book is indeed for the average woman who is hungry and wants more out of life. We will not accept that the good things in life, like wealth and affluence, are only for a select few. *No ma'am!* I want to show you that, yes, you can really have it all and do it all.

Consistent action, continual discussions and conversations, and information sharing can produce tremendous results for your financial outlook. It's about getting the right financial education and having that millionairess mindset. It's about developing the boldness to move beyond the things you've been taught and embracing the discernment and trust in your own financial gut.

Building wealth is a journey, not an event. Obtaining wealth doesn't happen overnight. It is a continual, perpetual thing. If you invest in yourself, dedicate time to get the information, submerge yourself in it, ask questions, and take action on what you've learned and the opportunities presented, you will begin to develop a new standard.

Are You Ready?

Maybe you can relate to my story and see yourself in similar circumstances that I have come out of. If you are a single parent or in a bad marriage, don't dwell on how hard it is because you have the ability to create your world with your words. Don't accept abuse, defeat, neglect, and deficiency as your destiny. Instead, use all that mess in your life as fertilizer for your personal and financial growth. I use my past experiences—good and bad—as building blocks for my life.

As you move through the pages of this book, I encourage you to speak the Millionairess Confessions I have placed in every chapter and in the appendix. There is power in your words. Gandhi said it best:

"Your beliefs become your thoughts,
Your thoughts become your words,
Your words become your actions,
Your actions become your habits,
Your habits become your values,
Your values become your destiny."

Isn't that so true?

If you are ready to break through what is holding you back, realign your wants with your actions, and arrive at your intention to reach and exceed your financial goals, join me on this amazing journey. While becoming a millionaire has a lot to do with the millions, it's even more about the person you have to become along the way. And that is what should excite you the most. Honey, you are on your way to holding your own in this world as a marvelous millionairess—to building a strong financial legacy for you and your family to move in the world the way it was intended from the start.

So without any more talk and little action, let's get this money!

Part One

MIND OVER MONEY

Chapter 1

Release the Millionairess

In order to get to the money, you've got to be willing to release the millionairess inside of you. On top of that, there are certain instincts that are cultivated based on culture, race, age, and gender. For example, there may be girls who naturally have an instinct for athletics...but they were pushed away from basketball or volleyball and pushed more toward cooking classes and ballet because of the gender roles reinforced around them. That decision had little to do with who they are on the inside and everything to do with their instincts being suppressed.

So, what happens is you have an instinct that's there, but because it was never cultivated, it never developed—which you can never benefit from. Because I grew up in a house of entrepreneurs, that instinct was there. This helped shape my view of money as a child. I didn't realize it, though, because growing up, I never had to work. Not even as a teenager. My parents and I never had conversations about me needing to get a job or needing to work for money. They didn't even put a demand on me to work for them. I was just living my life, going to school, having friends, and playing sports. I didn't get my first job until I was nineteen, when my parents basically lost everything.

I didn't realize I would naturally have a good work ethic. But since I watched my parents—and saw their behavioral patterns for a strong work ethic and success—when it was time for my first job, those instincts were activated. Because I saw my parents have a good work ethic all those years—working very long hours and always striving for success—everything just "turned on" for me, clicking into place.

I want every one of you to know that there is a millionairess inside of you. You just have to believe that you have the ability to become wealthy and that there are gifts in you. There are instincts in you, and you just need to get in the right environment so that they can be turned on. It's just like taking a fish out of water. If you take that fish out of water, eventually, it is going to die because it's not in the right environment. Same thing with polar bears—if you put a polar bear in a desert, it's not going to survive. For animals and humans alike, survival and success depend upon environment.

As a millionairess, you need to have an environment/community with others who celebrate your successes. An environment that allows you to hear things like "Great job," "You know what, that's your genius," "You know what, that's your brilliance," or, "You know what, you didn't understand everything, but you trusted your instincts." That's exactly why I created The Million-airess Club. I realized that even if a woman wants to be wealthy, if she's not in the right environment to cultivate how to think, how to move, or who to connect to, then it's not going to happen.

I've seen a lot of women whose husbands were intimidated by them making a lot of money or having success. They were so opposed to them letting their light shine. Instead of the wives saying, "You're going to have to work through that," they just shut down—which ended up inhibiting them from further growth. That's why I'm adamant about coaching women into releasing their millionairess, the one that's already on the inside. One way you are going to release your millionairess is by uprooting the wrong beliefs you have about money and establishing the right ones.

I know this isn't going to be easy. You've probably been thinking bad thoughts about money all your life. But you're not alone, and I don't expect you to divest yourself of those thoughts overnight. Researchers have said that for something to become a habit, you have to do it repeatedly every day, for at least twenty-one days. And that advice applies to creating small habits. So, trust me when I say: I know it may not be easy at first, but if you keep making small changes daily, you'll eventually change your mindset and your views about money.

This is done by debunking some of the things that you've thought or believed about money prior to now. I'm here to coach you through the process and help you release your inner million-airess. So, let's get to work uprooting bad beliefs and replacing them with the right beliefs.

EVOLUTION OF MONEY

Commodity Money (Barter System)	Metal Money (Gold / Silver / Copper)	Paper Money (By Gold / Government)	Plastic Money (By Institutions)	Digital Money (Centralized)	Digital Money (Decentralized)
---	700 BC	600+	1800+	1998	2008+

"Money is the root of all evil"

You may believe the quote above if you grew up in an impover-ished lifestyle. You may fear money because you know what it is like to not have enough and the ill treatment you receive when you don't have a certain amount of money. Or maybe you grew up in church or anywhere around church; if so, you've heard this quoted many times.

Though it may have been used to drive home a seemingly valid point in the midst of a sermon or a conversation, contextually, this quote has been misinterpreted for ages. As a result, you may think that people with money are evil. But the scripture clearly states that, "the love of money is the root of all evil," according to 1 Timothy 6:10. It is this kind of misinterpretation that can embed wrong beliefs about money into your mind.

As long as you keep your heart pure and don't make money a god, you're good. God is the One who gives you the power to receive wealth. If it was evil, why would He do that? You might as well be the one who it comes to pass through! Be a money conduit, and don't just let money pass through your hands.

Jewel's Gem

God is the One who gives you power to receive wealth.
If it was evil, why would He do that?

You may have thought or currently think the following:

- Money doesn't grow on trees.
- I have to be careful of what I buy.
- I have to wait on my husband/partner.
- I need to see what political party is going to be elected.
- I have to see what my boss is going to do.

If you start thinking you can never get out of the apartment, then nothing in you will say...*go look at a house*, or *go look at the mansion*, or *go drive your dream car*. This defeatist, self-fulfilling prophecy is like the plight of the independent slaves. They had the freedom to make their own way, but still decided to stay on the plantation because they felt that at least they knew they'd have a roof over their head and food on their table.

So that same mentality still exists generations later. You may say something like, "I'm okay. I'm doing okay. I'm doing alright." But there wasn't really an emphasis put on thriving or flourishing. You've been alright long enough. Now it's time to thrive, and you can start by being mindful of how you sow your money.

Below, you'll see how some wrong beliefs you may have can be uprooted and replaced with a millionairess's belief:

WRONG BELIEFS	MILLIONAIRESS BELIEFS
· Men handle money matters	· Money is a household matter
· I have no control over becoming wealthy	· I can have whatever I believe
· I don't have the money to invest	· Because I'm a good steward of my money, more money is attracted to me
· Starting a business is expensive	· Multiple streams of income improve my quality of life
· Money won't buy happiness	· I can upgrade to the life I want/desire
· Getting money is hard work	· When I solve problems, I'll always have money

"Money doesn't grow on trees"

This belief is adapted from the mindset that you should be careful about your spending, and that money is limited. I agree that you should be careful about your spending habits—you shouldn't be spending frivolously—but you do have to spend money to make money. For those of you who believe "money doesn't grow on trees," I beg to differ. To me, a tree is nothing more than a seed that was planted and matured over time. I've come across many different women who harbored this wrong belief about money, all because they were too afraid to believe in where they wanted to go.

Money sown in good ground or invested wisely always yields a harvest. If you want to make money, you can't be scared to spend some. Money is the seed, and the seed produces after its own kind. If you truly want to release your inner millionairess, not only do you have to uproot wrong mindsets about money, but you also have to get the seed in the ground. For that seed to produce, it has to be planted in the right environment. You can truly thrive when your environment is conducive for growth.

If there hasn't been an emphasis on thriving and flourishing present in your mind, then all roads lead back to the prevailing thought: "As long as I can take care of me and my kids." First of all, get rid of "as long as." What you should be saying is, "I'm going to be able to take care of myself, my children, and a city," or "myself, my children, and a whole community." Maybe even a whole nation, depending on how far you wanna go with this thing.

When I was a single mom, my goal was making sure I had a car that works. Now, years later, I'm giving away cars to single parents. Not only are all my cars debt free, but I'm giving cars away. But I had to cooperate with the Holy Spirit wanting to stretch me. And then, in addition to that, I had to connect with people who would stretch me. I had to connect with people who would not be impressed with where I was or the fact that I was just doing "okay." There's something about those relationships that can put a demand on your greatness; without them, you just kind of stall out where you are.

Jewel's Gem

A tree is nothing more than a seed that was planted and matured over time.

I would probably say 90 percent of the time, even today in 2021, I still hear a lot of, "My husband said he doesn't want to invest," "My husband said he doesn't want to do it," "My husband said not right now—maybe later." There's still a tremendous amount of authority given to husbands in the area of wealth education and investing, but it's because most women didn't grow up with parents saying, "You're going to do multiple million-dollar contracts," or "You're going to have your own wealth."

Yeah, you can marry a wealthy man—but you need to have your own wealth. You need to have your own money, and you need to be a great investor. You need to be able to make your own decisions about money. Growing up, that was never said to you. It was, more or less, "You're going to take the chicken out tonight," or "Did you sign little Johnny up for sports?" Most of the conversations that women have with their parents are very domesticated. All those conversations add up, subliminally sending a message that you don't belong on Wall Street. You don't belong in investing. You belong at home in the kitchen, taking care of the children. To some people, that's where you belong.

To change your mindset about money, you're going to need to read books that stretch you. Napoleon Hill's *Think and Grow Rich*, Kim Kiyosaki's *Rich Woman*, Thomas J. Stanley's *The Millionaire Next Door*, and my book *Millionairess Lifestyle* are some good starters. I strongly recommend getting into a wealth community (which can be researched on Google, Facebook, or Instagram or by joining The Millionairess Club) because so much about developing and becoming wealthy is in the conversations, the strategy, and the insights. You're going to really need a wealth community. Remain inquisitive. Ask tons of questions. Stay a student forever. Then you're going to have to make a decision that this is something that you're going to do. Women tend to like to do things in partnerships. We sometimes don't feel like we can go alone. But there are certain times you're going to have to go alone. Esther had to go alone. Ruth had to go alone. There are going to be times you have to go alone, too.

You can't always look to see what your husband thinks about it. I don't think there's anything wrong with asking your husband what he thinks about it, but I think that if his advice contradicts what you instinctively believe, then you need to do it. I can use myself as an example. Four years ago, when I started investing in Bitcoin, my husband was just like, "Oh, okay." Four years later, I've been able to build a really nice wealth portfolio because I made that decision for myself, even though he wasn't really too keen on it.

He didn't understand it. And if I would've needed his permission, I probably wouldn't have done it. Instinctively, he wasn't on board for doing it, but I trusted my financial instincts. The same thing happened with real estate. I've been able to build a really strong real estate portfolio in the inner cities. My husband comes from the inner city and has no interest in investing in the city of Detroit. So, if I had needed his approval to invest in real estate, I wouldn't have one property today because he hadn't wanted to do it.

I want you to understand that you can respect your husband, you can honor him, but the scripture talks about submitting to one another. You submit to your husband. What about him submitting to you? There has to be mutual respect for the instincts and the gifts present within your partner. He respects yours, and you respect his. It doesn't mean that if he doesn't want to do that, all your authority as a human being is taken away.

Sometimes, your beliefs about money can be shaped by what you were taught—or *not* taught—as a child or teenager. Growing up, money seemed like it was in endless supply to me. My parents wouldn't tell me "no" a lot. In my eyes, we were doing very well— we had nice stuff, housekeepers, and cooks. That wasn't common where I grew up. So my first viewpoint of money was that there was no limit—it was endless and always there. I knew Mommy and Daddy had it, and if I wanted it, I could have it.

But my beliefs changed somewhat, as I mentioned earlier, when we went through a financial loss when I was nineteen. I was devastated. I realized that we really didn't have it all together, and my viewpoint of wealth changed. It wasn't just the nice car, the nice house, and the nice things that were on my mind. I was starting to think about asset accumulation.

Over time, I realized that when money is being made, one of the best things you can do is pay yourself so that you can begin to accumulate assets...assets like real estate, oil, gold, and silver. Accumulating some of these things helps you get to a point where you can live off of the interest. if you invest in assets and are paid interest every month, eventually, you can keep building assets...and you can live off of the interest. So if your income disappears—for whatever reason—nothing is lost. You're a millionairess and were accumulating assets along the way.

If you aren't doing any asset accumulation and everything is about paying bills—even if the bills are paying off nice things—that's still not wealth. You have the appearance of wealth, but that's not real wealth. Real wealth is how much you have working for you if you decided to stop working tomorrow. What's that monthly amount that's coming in still? If there was no income, what's the interest that's coming in? That's where *real* wealth is built. You've got to be willing to make some tough decisions. You've got to realize that it's not going to necessarily be easy; it's going to take a level of perseverance and endurance.

Jewel's Gem

Real wealth is how much you have working for you
if you decided to stop working tomorrow.

You just have to make up in your mind that it's not going to be easy learning new principles. There are going to be distractions that come along. Whether it's little Johnny or big Joe or whoever, things are going to happen. But if you keep getting off of your original course of action, you're never going to make it across the finish line. Most people want to start the process, but once the process starts and it gets challenging or difficult or confusing, they quit.

My seventy-seven-year-old mother was investing for about a year; then she called and said she decided to quit. She was simply overwhelmed with learning one particular day. I couldn't understand why she hadn't reach out for help first. She's always wanted to understand investing, and she's approaching retirement. What happens is, most people don't want any kind of challenge. The minute there's a challenge, they're like, "I'm out." Thankfully, she eventually realized that quitting may not have been a smart decision. Although she was challenged at the moment, she decided to overcome that challenge by trying again. I'd argue that some people aren't used to using their brain. You may not necessarily use your intellect on a daily basis. Maybe you're used to using your hands. You may do hair, nails, personal training, wait tables—pretty much anything that mostly require your hands. By nature, people of color are particularly creative. But when it comes to investing, I'm talking about learning. Now you have to use a part of your brain that you haven't used in a long time, so your brain resists: *Stop it, stop it! I don't want this!* You've got to say, "I don't care what you want. You're going to learn." That's what the brain is for: to learn. This is really the decade of the brain, of learning, of education. You don't have to be ignorant. You can choose to learn.

MILLIONAIRESS-IN-THE-MAKING
· **Personality**: Authentically you (be willing to learn and grow)
· **Lifestyle**: Get used to upgrading your life across the board (throw away mismatched linens, towels, dishes, and so on)
· **Motives**: Change your life, your family's life, and your community
· **Beliefs**: I deserve it
· **Spending Habits**: Don't be cheap, but don't overspend (pay tithe and offering first; then you second)
· **Wealth-Building Strategies**: Something innovative with a component of tech in it; something that answers a problem for the future; nothing brick and mortar, but click and mortar; build your credit and build your capital

To get started, every day, you need to get up, determined that you're going to be a millionairess. Write out your goals and declare your affirmations—that part is huge. I journal every day, contemplating who I am and who I'm becoming. And then I say each of my goals and declarations out loud.

The next step is to start looking for my wealth community. Look for those collaborations or partnerships with people that can help you scale. Find a team that can help you scale, and they can take your vision and run with it. If you have those basic principles, it can be whatever business you want it to be, and you can win.

The biggest reason people don't win is because they're not confident. It's almost like you have two children. You tell both of the children, "After you're done playing today, whoever shows the most enthusiasm to finish this project and can talk about the project is going to win the prize." Well, I can see that the child who is more competent is the one who speaks well and shares their ideas and opinions. You're going to be sold because you're so impressed with how they communicate. So the number one thing to do, that we all have to do daily, is work on your self-confidence. If you feel confident about yourself, then you're going to feel good, and you're going to be more productive. If you don't feel good about yourself, you're going to constantly be second-guessing yourself...second-guessing if it's going to work, but really, you're second-guessing *your* ability to make it work. If that happens, your confidence is off. Your self-worth is off.

You need to work on more personal development so that you can become what you're wanting to be, as opposed to just being in love with an image, saying, *That's where I'm going, but I really don't understand the process yet because privately, I'm not there.* So, my goal is to get you there privately as much as possible; if you get there privately, then you're not going to have to convince the world of who you are. They're going to know because you're going to be living it out every day.

Your mindset really does impact what you believe about yourself. The way to shape your mindset is offering yourself affirmations, writing down goals, and forming relationships with people who celebrate your successes. These people can be honest with you but are authentic celebrators. There's nothing like hearing, "You are such a genius" from a peer, loved one, or friend. It affirms, like, "Yeah, I am a genius," "Oh my gosh, I am smart," "Oh wow, I can do that." So having relationships with people who are genuinely going to celebrate you, affirm you, and help push you out of your comfort zone is key.

If you change your beliefs, you change your actions. You're going to be much more aggressive. You're going to be a lot more aggressive toward a task that is put before you that's in your wheelhouse versus somebody saying, "Come over here and talk to me about private equity funds." In that situation, you're going to be like, "I'm way out of my league."

Jewel's Gem

If you change your beliefs, you change your actions.

So the more confident you are about a particular matter, especially when it comes to yourself, the bolder you're going to be in your own actions. With confidence, you'll feel better about it. Wealth communities provide you with the consistent education you need to obtain that confidence. To master money, you have to study it. You know the material, and at the end of the day, it just feels good to be like, "I know the material," and then deliver.

And now you manifest. And then, when you manifest, people are like, "Oh my gosh, you're amazing." You're like, "Yeah, because I manifest it." So then, guess what happens when everybody starts applauding you? It's going to boost your confidence, and then you're going to be able to go do it again.

Millionairess Confession: *I Am Courageous!*

Chapter 2

Stretch, Grow, and Go— Entering the Trust Zone

One important thing I had to learn recently is that being out of my comfort zone is an opportunity for me to stretch. I want to continue to grow and go to the next level, but in order to do that, I cannot be afraid to stretch.

Although it feels uncomfortable sometimes, and at times I feel like I'm going to choke, I keep pushing past the choking point. Everyone has a choking point where she feels like, "Oh my gosh! If I don't stop, I'll never be able to catch my breath." The good news is, when you push past the choking point, you experience growth. That's why I have grown to be more comfortable with stretching. It is now a part of who I am.

Stretching is supposed to be uncomfortable. So don't run away when you find yourself out of your comfort zone or when you're dealing with the unknown. You could be getting ready for the biggest breakthrough of your life. So learn to be comfortable with being uncomfortable. There are certain areas of my life where I have definitely become comfortable with being uncomfortable.

Jewel's Gem

Stretching is supposed to be uncomfortable. So don't run away when you find yourself out of your comfort zone.

All of us have that choking point, whether it's eating at a really nice restaurant or shopping at a Gucci store, saying, "I would never spend $1,200 on a purse." But then all of a sudden, you start making a lot more money and you're like, "I'm going to go do it for myself." Everybody has a choking point, and that choking point basically says, "I'm very uncomfortable with how I do things right now, but I'm making a decision that I'm going to start stretching in areas that I'm uncomfortable with."

Every single person has that. And the only way to stretch is just to do it. Pushing beyond your choking point allows you to raise the bar on your standard of living. Once you realize you deserve better, you're willing to go the extra mile to have better. You might as well get what you want now instead of living in regret later.

After moving past your choking point, you've increased your belief in what you can receive. Sometimes, you may find it easier to believe for other people, but you don't believe for yourself. But now, you've increased your belief on what you can have. You've increased your belief on what you deserve. And as a result, the money follows. Money follows vision—money *always* follows vision. That's why you have to work on your mindset every day. It's not a one-time thing. You've got to work on your mindset every day, so that these beliefs are ingrained in you and become a part of your lifestyle.

To refine your lifestyle, you should be studying people that have made millions of dollars doing what you want to do. Watch their YouTube videos. Buy their books. See if they have some type of mentorship program and get involved in it because there's always another level. You make a million, then you realize, why can't I make five? If you made five, why can't you make ten? If you make ten, why can't you make fifty?

Think about people who become billionaires. Unless it was inherited, they have to start at $1 million at some point, and they kept scaling through relationships and opportunities that provoked them to go to the next level.

Jewel's Gem

Money ALWAYS follows vision!

Being stretched into a new area in life requires living through and enduring growth pains. You have to be okay with this because you're being the trailblazer instead of the path finder. You're able to live through and to endure the growth pains because of those wealth relationships and wealth mentors. I don't know anybody who came into huge success, notoriety, money, or fame without enduring.

Glean from people who you admire. Again, watch people you want to be like; get on their YouTube channels and listen to what they have to say, read their books, go to classes. It's all about self-education. Most billionaires in 2020—while everybody was scared and watching Netflix and chilling—were reading. They were watching YouTube videos. They were self-educating. If you want to do this, you've got to go into massive self-education. When you hit a distraction or a stumbling block, you immediately think, "Challenge: quit." It has to be, "Challenge: work through"; or, "Challenge: find a solution"; "Challenge: think about it"; or, "Challenge: ask questions." It can't be "challenge and quit," 'cause otherwise, your goals are never gonna happen.

There's going to be pain whether you stay the same or change. Both can be painful. Both have their sets of challenges. The wealthy have their challenges, and the poor have their challenges. I'd rather have the challenges of the wealthy. Why not embrace positive pain? You have to realize that if you don't go through this painful experience of growth, then you're going to live with the pain of never changing, never increasing, or never reaching your goals.

You have to acknowledge that challenges are a part of life. They're not going to go away. You just have to make a decision that you're going to put yourself in a position to not remain stagnant and indecisive. The pain of staying the same is greater than the pain of growth. It's not a physical pain; it's discomfort. Remember, procrastination causes stagnation, and stagnation—bottom line— is little to no growth.

The world is changing so fast. If you couldn't keep up with Facebook and Instagram, you're definitely not going to be interested in Clubhouse (a social media platform that allows people from around the world to connect and discuss different topics via audio only). You're going to find yourself just becoming more obsolete and irrelevant. Do you realize there are million dollar deals being done on Clubhouse? Gayle King gets on there. Oprah gets on there. You can have audio conversations with some of your top influencers in the world and be given the tea on their strategies. You can end up really missing big waves because you wouldn't change—you keep overanalyzing. Don't get me wrong—I love analytical people. I have them on my team, and I need them.

But at the same time, you can overanalyze yourself right out of an opportunity.

By the time you decide to get on, you've missed the whole wave because you were thinking about it, or you were trying to look into it. Some things don't need to be looked into. They just need to be *jumped* into. And that really has to be your attitude. That's not going to be the same with everything, but your instinct will tell you, "You better jump." If you don't start jumping into some of these opportunities, you're going to become irrelevant. Your message—your brand—will become irrelevant. Your content might be amazing, but no one will know you exist.

You've got to stop being afraid of being disappointed. There are going to be days when you're going to really wish something hadn't happened, but you've got to stop counting your losses and focus on your wins. Do not be afraid of disappointment. That comes with the package. The longer you stay afraid, the more likely it is that you'll eventually look up and a whole year has gone by. You'll be in the same place and not have grown. It comes down to making a decision, and then you have to get with other jumpers. I've got jumpers in my life. And then I've got people who are looking into it in my life, but I have more jumpers than I have people looking into it, which has helped me to jump. Most of the time, anybody that works with me will tell you, I make a decision—usually within five minutes—if I'm going to do a deal or not.

Jewel's Gem

You've got to stop being afraid of being disappointed.

Stretching, growing, and going does require a certain level of trust on your part. Not only do you have to trust your instincts, but you also have to trust those around you. Be sure to hang out with people who love people and trust people at large. You know that everybody can't be trusted, but overall, you should expect the best from people. You should trust their gifts and their geniuses. When you meet somebody to do business with, listen for the genius. Listen for the brilliance. Don't listen to see if they may make a mistake here or if they're not perfect there. Look to hear any areas that could possibly be advanced and promoted.

The old school mindset is not to trust anybody. A lot of people were taught not to trust, and as a result, they don't have the money, connections, investment opportunities, or lifestyles they desire. What happens is, you end up distrusting in *every* area. If lack of trust causes you to miss out on an opportunity, the loss is always greater on the backend because one opportunity always leads to another. Deciding to learn how to trade five years ago has opened up so many doors since I started. Had I missed out on one opportunity, I probably would've missed out on many others.

Most wealthy people trust automatically. They take you at your word. Start trusting, but don't override if your instinct is saying, "Don't do business with them." Don't! But keep in mind— that can't be the response with everything. Trusting comes down to believing in your instincts and your discernment. When you talk to people, listen for the voice *behind* the voice—what vibes you are getting from them. And then if you feel like you can trust them, move forward with the deal. If you can't, something in your gut will tell you they're not trustworthy. A lot of it is your instinct—but don't just assume that somebody can't be trusted because they're sharing with you something that you don't know. And again, it doesn't mean you should give them all your money. But at least be open to discussion.

When you have developed a reputation of distrust with your-self, it causes a lack of growth, a lack of confidence, which leads to stagnation. Trusting positions you for prospects that will open up other prospects—which will bring more increase, more revelation, more understanding, and more insight. Next thing you know, you're wide open to growth because trust is no longer an issue, and how you do one thing is how you will do everything.

Jewel's Gem

How you do one thing is how you will do everything.

I remember when the opportunity came for me to host *The Jewel Tankard Show.* I was so grateful and excited. My own show! Then I found out that I had to do everything for the show. I had to create a team to put the show together, and I had to do it by faith. I could have easily said, "Since all of the pieces of the puzzle are not together, I'm just not going to move forward with it because I don't know what I'm doing." I was definitely out of my comfort zone. However, God helped me and brought all the pieces together. As a result, I continued to stretch. I continued to live by faith, even though there were times I felt uncomfortable.

The first season of the show was amazing. For the show's second season, I knew I needed to move to Atlanta. Once again, I became uncomfortable, wondering about all the details concerning the move to Atlanta like, "What am I going to need?" and "How much is it going to cost?" I was looking and asking questions, but nothing seemed to fit. Then, all of a sudden, every-thing fell into place. What if, in the middle of my discomfort, I had stopped? Although I was way outside my comfort zone, I kept moving forward. I didn't stop, and things began to change and line up. My point is, I would not have made it this far if I hadn't followed my gut—if I had been afraid to be uncomfortable.

The key to being comfortable when you are outside your comfort zone is to have emotional intelligence, which is the ability to read and monitor your own emotions as well as the emotions of others. When you increase your emotional intelligence, you will increase your finances, too, because when you have self-control, you will be kind and patient with people. That is what people will remember about you, and that is what will cause them to want to partner with you. People like to partner with people they feel they can trust emotionally.

God gave us emotions, but I never want my negative emotions to control me—anger, frustration, and impatience. I want to display compassion, love, forgiveness, discernment, and discretion. I want my discernment—not my feelings—to rule and reign in my decision-making. Also, I don't give myself permission to engage in negative emotions over something that I might see as potentially disappointing, discouraging, or hurtful. At night, before I go to bed, I confess: "I go to bed in peace, and I wake up in prosperity."

On my Jumpstart chart opposite, there are some things you can do that will help you maintain comfort when outside of your comfort zone.

Maintaining trust when being stretched outside of your comfort zone isn't easy. However, it can be done. You just have to be willing to discipline yourself for it.

Millionairess Confession: *I Am Unstoppable!*

JEWEL'S JUMPSTART

1. **Manage your emotions.** This is so important. Always allow enough time to go by so you can gain control of your emotions before you make a move. Never allow your emotions to lead you in a direction you do not want to go in.

2. **Don't ask everybody what they think about you stepping out of your comfort zone in order to accomplish something big.** The average person has a poverty mentality and won't understand your giant-sized dream.

3. **Make problem solving a part of your daily activities.** Successful people have the ability to solve their problems and the problems of others, and they manage their emotions in the process. The bigger the problems you have, the more money you will make.

4. **Whenever you begin to feel overwhelmed, take the time to walk away from your desk and those around you.** Find a quiet place to just sit and think. By doing so, you will avoid making decisions based on your emotions.

Chapter 3

Goal Digger, Goal Getter

If you obsess with personal discipline, then the public reward will come. Private growth is more important than public recognition because private growth will eventually overflow into what the public sees and knows about you. For example, you can't keep getting on social media, saying you're about to lose fifty pounds and then never change the way you eat, what time you eat, or your gym routine. Publicly, what you want to display is never going to catch up.

Success is something that we should be able to measure. That's why it's important to be honest with yourself and assess where you are when you find yourself at the end of your capacity. For instance, you may realize that it's time to bring on another team member or hire a housekeeper, an accounting firm, a marketing team, or a social media team. When you assess where you are, you will know where you need to be.

I like to write down my daily goals, do a vision board, and create new disciplines—like writing down daily confessions. I have over one hundred confessions that cover every area of my life. I make confessions about being a great wife, investor, teacher, CEO, and strategist. I also confess that I am anointed, beautiful, smart, bold, courageous, and unstoppable. Habakkuk 2:2 says, "Write the vision, and make it plain upon tables, that he may run that readeth it." Very successful people spend time writing down their goals.

We all have many responsibilities and many different things coming at us in the course of a day. We tend to get bombarded by life, and as a result, we lose our course. I remember when I wanted to start my own dish line. I wanted the words "I am a millionairess" written on them. So, I wrote it down as a goal, and it became a part of my vision. Also, I started making confessions about my dish line, which kept it at the forefront of my mind.

The next thing I did was contact a gentleman in New York that I believed could get the dishes manufactured. His name is Steve. During our conversation, he said, "Yeah, I think I can do it." He started the research and development (R&D) process to see who would be the best person for the job at the best price.

It took him about a month to get things in order. During that time, I continued making my confessions, and I made contacting him a weekly goal. Steve found a vendor, and we got the samples together and tweaked them. Still focusing on my vision and making confessions, I followed up with him every step of the way. Finally, the dishes were being made. After they were made, I had to get them shipped. I had some issues because they were being shipped internationally. However, because this project was part of my weekly goals, was on my vision board, and was part of my daily confessions, it stayed before me and didn't become another good idea that ended up on the shelf. Instead, I made the necessary moves toward accomplishing that goal.

I am sharing this because I want you to know that you can be a strong finisher. You don't have to be like so many people who start projects but never finish them. Just remember, there is a process. You have to go through phase one, then phase two, then phase three, and phase four. Then, once you have established your brand, product, or business, you need to be ready and willing to reinvent yourself—be willing to evolve and innovate for enhancement when necessary.

Hewlett Packard is a good example of a company that has successfully reinvented itself. The company started out selling huge printers. However, over the years, their printers have been getting smaller and smaller, to the point where we can now print from our cell phones. This company wouldn't be around today if they hadn't continued to develop and evolve.

In order to achieve great success, you have to reset your standard and create greater disciplines for yourself. Don't be afraid to raise the bar. Perhaps there are things you are not doing now that you should start doing.

Another example I want to share with you is something many of us struggle with on a daily basis, and that's managing our weight. I went through a period when I was struggling to lose ten pounds. One day, while hanging out with my sister, she said, "Jewel, you're still picking up pounds from eating carbs." I told her that I didn't eat that many carbs, and she reminded me how often I was eating jalapeno chips. She said, "Every time you pick up those jalapeno chips, even though they are organic, you're still eating carbs." So, I knew I needed to become more conscious about eating carbs, which meant I had to create new disciplines and consider new snacks.

Jewel's Gem

In order to achieve great success, you have to reset your standard and create greater disciplines for yourself.

You see, my personal life isn't that much different from my business life when it comes to creating new disciplines. I've learned to be willing to create new disciplines as I expand. As a result, I have achieved a whole new level of growth. I've also learned that with growth comes more responsibility and greater discipline.

Over time, I have become very focused on my confessions and disciplines. I have not mastered this yet, but I'm growing in the process. As a result, I have gotten better at narrowing down projects and have become very selective when it comes to taking on new ones. If I am going to be disciplined where my current projects are concerned so I can reach my end goal for them, I can't afford to be all over the place.

Jewel's Gem

With growth comes more responsibility and more discipline.

I encourage you to narrow down your goals—focus and hone in on where you are and what you are doing. Whether you are in the beginning, intermediate, or advanced stage of your business or career, you need to look at where you are and then where you need to be.

The following is further insight on the value of setting goals, presented by Asheia Wynne Léonard, CCO of The Jewel Tankard Brand, who spoke to the members of The Millionairess Club on focusing on and narrowing down their goals. I am sure it will help you, too:

"*You want to be honest about the things that are keeping you from accomplishing your goals and coming up with solutions. I think having that conversation is the nuts and bolts that will get you unstuck so you can have some movement. It could be that you need some help. So, maybe hiring a housekeeper would free up the hours you need every week to focus on your business. Or, if you're feeling too tired, start working out or taking B_{12} vitamins to get your energy up. You can't just say, 'I'm working a 9 to 5, and as soon as I get home, I'm too tired.' Instead, ask yourself, 'What am I going to do about it?' This is the place where you come face-to-face with those things that could hinder you from accomplishing your goals and meet them head-on.*

"*Another important thing is to take fast action. For instance, what steps will you take within the next 24 hours to get started on your goals? This is important because many times we get stuck in analysis paralysis, where we feel like if everything hasn't been figured out, then we can't get started.*

"*For example, I had this amazing idea to create an app. It is a revolutionary, life-changing app that is sure to have me on the cover of Forbes. Immediately, I had to figure out what I could do right away to get started. I didn't want to allow myself to think that it was impossible to do. So, the first thing I did was look online to see if there were any other apps like the one I wanted to create. I didn't want to invent the wheel if I didn't* have to. I could look at what is already out there, tweak it, and make it better. Then I wrote down my idea and concept and looked for someone to create a logo. These were my fast-action steps that I started on immediately. I needed to see that I was making progress.

"You must always be in a position where you are putting forth action. You will feel so amazing when you see the little pieces come together. You will have little victories as well as build momentum. You'll be like, 'Yes! I'm one step closer.'

Now, when it comes to setting goals, you don't want your goals to be all over the place. If you have a goal set to accomplish in the next month, it should be something that is aligned with your three-month goal. Likewise, if you have a goal set to accomplish in three months, it should be aligned with your six-month goal. For instance, if you have a goal to be debt free, your one-month goal should be to pay off your credit cards bills. Your three-month goal should be to pay off your car. Each thing feeds into the overall goal of becoming debt free. In other words, your one-month goal should be a smaller step toward your three-month goal, and your three-month goal should be a small step toward your six-month goal. This way, you shouldn't feel overwhelmed while accomplishing your overall goal.

"Goals can also be items you want to purchase. There-fore, you must have money goals. It is important to know that enormous wealth is created by what you do with your money. You don't want to just make money; you want to multiply it. However, it is all about your thought process. It is what separates the wealthy from those who are not wealthy, and the middle class from the upper class. When money hits my account, the first thing I ask is, 'Will I purchase something or invest it?' I have trained myself to think of ways I can experience growth, multiplication, increase, and duplication.

"So, it is wise to invest a percentage of your income. Think of yourself as a money-making machine. It's like a snowball effect, and you see your money multiplying massively because you've invested in various money multiplication systems. One year, I invested 15 percent of my income, and the following year I increased it to 25 percent. That was a 10-percent growth in the amount I invested, but it was also an increase in my returns.

"The average person doesn't understand the importance of having specific money goals. They have not grown enough in the matters of money to even consider how much they have grown financially from a percentage standpoint. Instead, they just look at how much money they have without ever considering asking themselves if they are really growing financially or if they are regressing.

"When I transitioned from working in corporate America to becoming a full-time entrepreneur/investor, I had to look at my cash flow and portfolio. I had to ask myself how my money was growing from an investment standpoint. Or, how well was my money growing from my business and investments? I decided that I wanted to grow my personal bank account by XYZ percent to equal blank dollars. Then I wanted to grow my business bank account by X percent to equal blank dollars and invest X percent of income.

"At some point, we should get to the place where our investment income is equal to our business income or it is equal to our salary. When our investment income is equal to our salary, we are at the point where we can live off of the interest, and we won't have to touch the principle.

"All of this begins with setting and accomplishing business and money goals, changing your thought process, and managing your growth."

Every goal needs a deadline, so that you don't have the same goal for ten years. Use dates, and then use deadlines, and then make sure that you keep making your goals bigger every year—which puts a demand on you to grow. I would write those dates down, write the deadlines down, write down what the goal is, and then work backwards. So the goal is this, but what are the action steps that need to happen on a daily basis? Because most goals are going to require consistency. So you have to figure out what you need to be doing every day to reach this end goal. So, in a nutshell: dates, deadlines, the goal, and then the action steps—the daily tasks that are required to make that goal happen.

Jewel's Gem

Every goal needs a deadline.

Financially, set three goals—one year, five year, and ten year—and place parameters around your goals so that you can accurately measure the success. Be honest with yourself and ask, "How much am I willing to work towards this goal?" Before setting goals, find out what you really love to do that's also income producing. It can't just be a hobby—you've got to be able to turn it into revenue. Other than asking yourself, "Is this income producing?," firstly, you should be tithing and then paying yourself—looking for appreciating assets that will add value over time—buying.

JEWEL'S JUMPSTART
· Tithe
· Pay yourself
· Don't overspend
· Decrease debt (while also investing)

Sometimes, all you need is a boost in the right direction. A metamorphosis to millionairess status does not happen overnight, but it is sure to happen when you reset your standard and create greater disciplines for yourself and when you aren't afraid to raise the bar and reinvent yourself. Self-care is key when reinventing yourself.

Millionairess Confession: *I Am Bold!*

Chapter 4

The Importance of Self-Care

Mastering your mind, body, and spirit are essential to your success as a millionairess and central to building and sustaining your empire. Exercise is very important. It keeps us healthy and increases our energy level.

I recently got a membership at Planet Fitness. They have an LED light that goes over your entire body, including your face. It's called the Beauty Angel. It actually causes the collagen to pop on your skin. As we get older, we start to lose collagen, and now there's an LED light that helps to pop it. I stay in this light for twelve minutes. It helps with muscle groups like legs, arms, abs, and glutes, and it also helps to reduce stress and energize, giving the body a twelve-minute workout. After I get that LED light on my face, I notice that my skin looks firm, tight, and plump.

I also go to the Hand and Stone Massage and Facial Spa for their LED light once a month. They have locations all over the country. I believe a membership there is around seventy dollars a month. All of this is part of my brand.

Here are a few personal cosmetic tips I want to share with you that will help you feel more physically confident as you pursue your business or career:

1. Take time to go through your clothes. This is something I do often. Although I am a big investor, I have to admit that I am also a shopper. However, I am somewhat of a bargain shopper. I try to be mindful of how much money I spend. I am very frugal, and I spend very little in comparison to what I make. So, when I go through my closet, I pull out clothes that I know I am not going to wear anymore and give them away. I have a funnel system of old clothes going out and new clothes coming in. By doing this, I stay with the trends. This is very important because as a woman, it gives me leverage.

2. When looking for stylish and trendy clothes, a good place to start is on Pinterest. It is a great place to get some ideas on clothes, makeup, and much more.

3. Throw out old washcloths and towels, especially once they become mismatched, tattered, or have holes in them. Having those old ones around will play with your psyche. So, do yourself a favor and go buy new ones.

4. If you are not going to do a full face of make-up, be sure to at least wear eyeliner and lip gloss. You always want your eyes to look good, and you never want to show up anywhere with chapped lips.

5. Make sure your shoes are up-to-date. See which ones are beat up on the heel or are simply outdated. Then decide which ones you want to keep and which ones you want to give away. You have to make room for new shoes.

6. I wear a waist trainer or spandex almost every day and recommend them both if you want a confidence boost. You don't want to get used to walking around looking sloppy.

7. If you wear glasses, release your faith to get a pair of Gucci glasses. I was not into designer names at first, but as I made more money and my circle grew wider, it became a big deal. Multimillion-dollar brands know about designer items. To them, it's a status symbol. So, pick up one or two designer pieces to wear when you go into a boardroom to negotiate. Even though designer labels don't mean you're wealthy, wearing them will demand a certain amount of respect from the people you are doing business with. They won't feel like you are begging. They will know you are solid.

8. Dental work is also very important to your brand. You may need to get braces, whitening solution, whitening toothpaste, or even go to a dentist to have your teeth whitened. Whatever the case may be, do it. I get my teeth whitened once a year, and I used to wear braces because my teeth were shifting. I just got them removed a few years ago.

Be mindful that being smart, intelligent, stylish, and trendy are the things that will give you leverage at the negotiating table.

Now, I want to approach the topic of hair. As women of color, we have so many wonderful alternatives when it comes to having a beautiful head of hair. Terry, who is the owner of Bella J. Hair, shared some very important information and tips with The Millionairess Club members. Here's what she had to say:

"When it comes to my hair, I am all natural. However, after working out, it is sometimes hard to look my best. My hair doesn't want to cooperate. Since I don't want to use chemicals

on my hair, I found myself flat ironing it every day. Then I started using various products, especially gel, to smooth and slick my edges. However, gel has a lot of alcohol in it, and it causes alopecia.

"Both my aunt and my business partner's aunt had breast cancer. I also had several members in my family who were suffering from alopecia. As I began having conversations with these and other women who were experiencing the effects of alopecia and those who were losing their hair due to cancer treatments, I decided to come up with a solution.

"So, I started selling hair. However, my focus isn't always on making money from selling hair. I also want to help educate women so they will know that they can still be natural and have an alternative that will give them the look and the professionalism needed when they have to attend business meetings or appear on the red carpet. I want women to know that they have options.

"My weaves and hair extensions are Malaysian, Brazilian, and Burmese. It is 8A grade hair, which is a premium grade, 100-percent virgin, unprocessed, human Remy hair. With proper care, it can last up to two years. All of the cuticles are intact, and it can be colored twenty different ways. I also carry bundles and closures, and we do custom wigs. However, the wigs are very expensive because they are put together with what is called a 360 bundle, and the 360 is open. In other words, it's like the middle of your head is open, and the wig goes completely around it. It is seamless. Therefore, you have the seamless look all the way around your head. Believe me, the 360 Frontal wig is life! And depending on the technique of the stylist, you can leave the 360s in for about 4 to 5 weeks.

"I recommend asking your stylist if they have had experience installing frontals, lace frontals, or lace 360s. If the stylist has no experience, then you are taking a chance and may lose your edges. So make sure you have an experienced stylist to do your installation.

"As I previously stated, I want to be a blessing and teach women about buying the right hair, how to install the right hair, and how to take care of it so they can do their thing with their hair looking fabulous. Your hair is your crown and glory, so you've got to take care of it.

"Anyone interested in contacting me for more information can visit my website at www.bellajhair.com."

The information Terry shared with our club members was really valuable, especially to the ones who were looking for alternatives to using chemicals or flat ironing their hair every day. Although we want our hair to look fabulous, we don't want to harm it in the process. Going natural and wearing weaves or extensions are ways to ensure that your hair looks fabulous every day while conducting business.

I highly recommend Bella J. Hair. I am a happy customer, and my favorite is the Brazilian hair. It is so beautiful, and I love it! With so many alternatives and choices available, no woman who is trying to be at her best should ever have a "bad hair day."

I think the number one thing is every day I'm endeavoring to be my best self. And I think most successful people have a very strong focus on personal self-development and being physically, emotionally, and mentally well in every area of their lives. If you don't put enough focus there, your self-care will be poor.

Some people don't take care of themselves because they have value issues. They don't love themselves. You show love for yourself by how you treat yourself—it's reflective. For example, last year, I found out that my sugar levels were elevated. I immediately snatched sugar out of my diet, including fruit. Now, did I miss it? Did I want it? Yeah. But I wanted to be healthy more than I wanted something sweet.

So self-care takes a lot of discipline. And I think sometimes we go to foods or different substances because of how we manage life or perceived pressure, but all pressure is perception. So somebody can live in a trailer and drive a basic car and feel like they're under pressure. Somebody can live in a mansion and have luxury cars and feel like they're under pressure. It's all perception. *You* control that. One of the biggest things that I think is important in becoming a millionairess is becoming extremely self-aware and then controlling those areas of your life.

Most people feel helpless—feeling like they can't control their weight, they can't control what they think about, and they can't control what they feel. Growing up, you weren't taught, "Oh, you can control your thoughts." Nobody heard that or "You can control how you feel." Most of the time, people grow up like they're helpless, and they can't control how they feel or what they think about. It becomes hard for a person to master money if they can't master themselves.

So, the number one goal for somebody who desires to be wealthy is self-mastery, which means that you work on yourself every day. You're doing personal development. You're listening to things that make you better. You're having conversations that make you better. You're eating things that make you better. You're thinking things that make you better. One thing about it: the more you practice what you think about and practice how you feel, the more you realize you can do it.

Jewel's Gem 💎

The number one goal for somebody who desires to be wealthy is self-mastery.

If you go through life thinking you can't control these things, then you allow your life to be controlled from the outside in, and that's tormenting. If the outside isn't lining up with what you think is an ideal life, then your expectations seem unreal. You might begin doubting if you're actually able to be successful. Real success is not allowing the outside to control the inside. Real success is allowing the inside to determine the outside. And that takes practice. It takes community. It takes the Word of God. And you definitely have to be intentional. If you're not intentional, then you'll just kind of wake up and say, "Oh, we'll see what happens today." Or, "As long as nobody else says something, or as long as nobody else does something, then I'm going to be fine." But that's the problem. Because you're basically giving people authority in your life to determine how you feel, how you move, and what you decide to do. When you do that, you suffer the consequences.

Most people aren't raised with the concept of self-mastery. So it does take time to recode or reprogram how you think. That's a big deal, but I practice this on small stuff. When you decide to start being more self-aware, the biggest thing that you have to become aware of is: What are you thinking? What are you feeling and why? And then reprogram yourself and say, "I don't give this person authority over my life." You're basically taking back control and realizing that no one can make you do anything.

When people don't practice self-awareness, they usually have self-destructive behavior because they're giving other people the authority to manipulate and control their emotions and thoughts. But really, nobody can do that unless you give it to them. That's power that has to be given.

With more success comes more responsibility. And it's hard to be responsible if you're not in good health and a good place with yourself. So that's why self-awareness is a really big deal. Now, if you look at people who are in a leadership position, you usually don't know if they've had a bad day. Think about when President Obama was in office—you never heard him get up and say, "You know, I fell out with my cousin really bad last night. I'm going to need to take a couple of hours." It doesn't mean that he doesn't have those issues. What it *does* tell us is that he has gained a great deal of self-mastery, which allows him to be in a position to be able to run a country. You cannot run anybody else's life if you cannot run your own.

Jewel's Gem

When people don't practice self-awareness, they usually have self-destructive behavior.

Sometimes, you have people who want big success. They want to have empowerment movements, but the first person you have to empower is yourself. What's most important is, if you want to have a strong brand of empowerment or wealth building, then it needs to be reflective in your life. That doesn't mean you have to be perfect by any means—but it does mean that there has to be some level of maturity, emotionally and mentally, that qualifies someone to say, "I'm going to pay you every day, or every week, or every month, to coach me or give me direction because I see that there's clear direction in your life."

Practical Self-Care

I take all the vitamins. I actually have a nurse who comes over every month and gives me infusions; it's what they call a Midas cocktail—Vitamins B, C, and D. Then, I get hydrogen peroxide—it puts oxygen back into the body, and it kills all viruses and diseases right on contact.

Like I mentioned previously, I also have a membership with the Hand and Stone Spa. I go there every month to get a two-hour deep tissue massage and facial. And then, I have a hairdresser who comes over to my house to do my hair. I also have a massage therapist who comes over once a month to do two-hour deep tissue massages. Self-care is all about setting yourself up to work smart.

I work fourteen-hour days, and I love what I do. I wouldn't change it. But I also have a very high acumen for taking care of myself. Most people need time off, but I thrive off of working. As a result, I'm heavy on the self-care.

Wealth is not just money. It's also the ability to create a support system. It's the ability to create things that add value to your life, which help you to relax and stay clear and feel good. If your mind is not clear, it's going to be tough to make decisions. Conversely, if your mind is clear but your body is tired, you're not going to be motivated to do anything.

Lastly, your spirit needs to be alert so that discernment can kick in. They really need to all be functioning at a very high capacity so that you can be free to move and flow. There's nothing worse than having to work when you're tired or work when you're exhausted—whether that's mentally or emotionally. Daily, I put myself in a position to do things that make sure I feel good.

Jewel's Gem 💎

If your mind is not clear,
it's going to be tough to make decisions.

Although I do love shopping and I do consider retail therapy as a form of self-care, my biggest thing is making sure that I'm accumulating assets as opposed to spending money frivolously. Everything goes back to your value system. If I'm not healthy emotionally, mentally, or physically, then my world is not going to be good. Getting a massage a couple times a month, me getting infusions—all of these things set me up for success. If you can't stop to invest in you, then you're too busy. You can't change the world if you're broken or fragmented. Here's the bottom line: the more personal responsibility you take for your life, the more likely it is for you to win, and win *really* big. People who win really big are creatures of habit.

Stress Management

Pressure and stress are all perceptions. You can say at any given time, "I'm under a lot of pressure." Again, it goes back to what you think about yourself and what you think about your life. For example, I have quite a few rental properties. Because of Covid-19, I have tenants that are paying. I have tenants that need to be evicted. I have tenants that are obnoxious. I have some tenants that are nice, but I have some that are obnoxious and racist. In fact, one of my tenants happens to be a racist. Do I really care that he's a racist? Not really, as long as he pays every month. So all of those different factors are going on, but I've already made a decision that I'm going to focus on the fact that I own the property free and clear.

I'm grateful that the rental properties have brought some profits. Instead of being stressed, I'm just focused on the fact that I'm a property owner and a black woman in the city where I came from. I'm a part of economic revitalization. I could be complaining about the work associated with these properties—taxes, upkeep, maintenance—and sometimes I catch myself getting ready to go there. Then I think, be grateful you have them. Be grateful you have the titles for them. *Be grateful!* So I always snatch myself back with extreme amounts of gratitude—which makes me be a much happier person. You're never going to talk to me and find me in a bad mood.

To better help you manage stress, you should be working on your perception every day. You can combat it by exercising and drinking a lot of water also, but a lot of stress is mental. You can literally talk yourself out of being stressed out, just like you can talk yourself *into* being stressed out. Always practice extreme amounts of gratitude, and then pull from everything you're grateful for. When you're busy being grateful, you don't have time to be stressed.

Emotional Health and Balance

People like to do business with nice people. People like to do business with people who are emotionally stable. If you see someone who may have potential but you see that they're emotionally unstable, it may make you second-guess doing business with them. You have to be willing to be the kind of person who you want to do business with. You can't be talking empowerment one month, and then the next month, you hate everyone or you're thinking, "I wanted to kill somebody today," or just having self-doubt. Although it might be true, it's not a brand that people will consider solid. If you really want to acquire wealth, then how people perceive you is important. Again, it's emotional intelligence—become aware of what you're feeling, why you're feeling it, and then change it if necessary.

According to helpguide.org, "effective stress management helps you break the hold stress has on your life, so you can be happier, healthier, and more productive. The ultimate goal is a balanced life, with time for work, relationships, relaxation, and fun—and the resilience to hold up under pressure and meet challenges head on." You can practice stress management by journaling those emotions and then asking the people around you how they handle stress. How do you handle when something happens that you don't like?

Jewel's Gem

People like to do business with nice people.

I think that balance is overrated. I think that people don't need to look for balance when they're building an empire. But if you are trying to find it, you've got to discover what works best for you. What works for one person may not work for the next. There are times when I work ten to fourteen-hour days, and while some people couldn't do it, I love it. Balance can be elusive at times, so you have to do what works for you and makes you happy. When you're an overachiever, you're not fighting for balance—you're fighting for fulfilment and achieving goals.

You've got to do what works for you, and you've got to be okay with working long hours for particular seasons of your life. You're building an empire. This is going to take a substantial amount of work—not necessarily labor, but it's going to take work, and it's not going to happen overnight. So you can't aim to be average. You got to be okay with being an overachiever and find a happy place. That's why I do all those extra self-care things—because they make me happy.

Positive Body Image and Physical Exercise

A lot of times, people decide if they're going to do business with you based on how you look—how you take care of yourself physically, if they smell you or not in a meeting, what your hygiene is like, and even your dental care. You've got to have your mouth together. You've got to go to the dentist. You've got to be getting your teeth cleaned. You've got to floss. All that stuff matters.

A lot of people hate on the Kardashians, but really, the Kardashians just invested a lot into self-care, body image, and body wear because basically, their brand has been built on them keeping themselves together. Honestly, you look at people like Naomi Campbell—she still looks really good. I saw a picture of her, and she looked like she's about thirty-five, and she's fifty years old.

For the most part, very few people make it to those levels. It's not this way in all cases, but sometimes, you've got somebody who's got a lot of money, but they're mentally off. Or you've got somebody who's got a lot of money, but they still deal with heavy depression. Some celebrities that seemingly have it all end up committing suicide or having suicidal thoughts. This is why I put a lot of focus on getting the package. Don't just get the bag because the bag without a sound mind—the bag without looking good, feeling good—is *not* good. Your mental health is connected to everything, especially when it comes to wealth and business. You really, authentically want to feel good. You want to authentically look good. Then it's going to project. You won't have to worry about any part of your brand being fake.

Body image is very important, but I wouldn't want anybody to take it to extremes. I wouldn't want everybody to *just* focus on body image, but inside, they're really depressed. I wouldn't want anybody to focus on really great hygiene, body image, and getting the right bag, but mentally be struggling. I'm really about trying to get the whole package. You know, when Jesus died, He didn't just die for our salvation. He didn't just die for deliverance. He didn't just die for us to be rich. He didn't just die for us to be healed. He literally died for us to be rich, to be healed, to be whole, and to be delivered. You really can have the whole package. It's going to take work, but it's definitely achievable.

Bible Study and Prayer

All success principles come from the Bible—every single one. There are over 2,500 scriptures that discuss money. That whole wealth piece is strong. The whole Biblical piece is strong because it deals with your joy. It deals with peace being made available because of the Word of God. Joy has been made available because of the Word of God. Prosperity has been made available. Good relationships have been made available because of the Word of God. Getting your eyes on the Word of God is important. Get those scriptures in every day, even if it's one scripture.

I am also a strong proponent of having a church home, not just church-hopping. It stabilizes you spiritually, knowing God has called you to a specific place where He's designated you to grow.

Prayer unlocks the secrets and mysteries. When you pray, it releases the mysteries of God. The secret things that would be hidden. You could almost say it's hidden for you but not from you.

God has to be the Source. Businesses will come and go, and deals will come and go, and investments will come and go. A lot of that stuff is forever changing and moving. You want to make sure you put yourself in a position where God is your Source. Imagine, you have a business partner you did business with for a long time—when, all of a sudden, that business partnership is over for whatever reason. Everything worldly has a cycle and a season. But when God is your Source, He keeps you from going off balance when life cycles show up.

So, prayer unfolds. It reveals. It guides and directs, and it keeps the main thing, *the main thing*. Always remember that God is your Source, and trust Him with your life, your family, your business, and your investments. So, when things happen externally, you're not thrown because you've developed a strong relationship with God as your Source.

Positive Confessions, Affirmations, and Meditation

Positive confessions are really good. Whatever you meditate on, you become. It's good not to just say things, but write them down. Also, make sure that your conversations do not contradict what you are confessing. You've got to make sure that your confessions and your conversations are in alignment. Now, that doesn't mean that you can't have authentic conversations. There's nothing wrong with that. But you've got to make sure you're not making these positive confessions, and then getting on the phone with your girlfriends, saying the opposite of what you've been confessing.

Jewel's Gem 💎

You've got to make sure that your confessions and your conversations are in alignment.

Your private life and your public life need to merge. Again, that doesn't mean you can't have time to have authentic conversations—but you've got to make sure that what you say, you believe. If you believe in those confessions, then they'll come out in your relaxed conversations. They don't need to be totally separate. There needs to be congruency. When people see you in public, it should be the same person you are privately. It shouldn't be two separate entities, because you're going to manifest what you say and what you believe—which is why every day, you need to be working on your belief: Belief in the Word of God. Belief in the vision that God has given you. Belief in the dream that He's given you.

Millionairess Confession: *I Am Worthy!*

Part Two

MONEY ON YOUR MIND

Chapter 5

Embrace the New Rules for Your Money

Wealth education is not just for the privileged; it's for the hungry, the teachable—whoever is ready to stretch, grow, and go. Wealth is a mindset and skillset. More than just financial literacy, in this book, you'll gain key insight on some of the new pathways to wealth. The days of sitting down with your financial planner and saying, "Okay, I'm going to just give you my money, and you go and do whatever you think is best," are over.

Now it's all about self-education. Self-education is extremely important right now. And while educating yourself on CDs, bonds, and mutual funds is good…you don't become wealthy just because of that. You have to join wealth educational communities. You have to learn the modern approaches. You really have to put yourself in a position to learn new things. I'm not saying don't have a 401k, or don't invest in CDs or bonds. What I am saying is that the investments routes that worked for your grandparents are very, very slow and very, very antiquated. When you look at a bond, those things pay maybe 2 or 3 percent for the year. Now, we have investments that'll pay that in a *day* with foreign exchange, cryptocurrency, binary options, as well as some stocks. That's really what you want to think about now.

You want to put yourself in a position to manage that money. You can start with very little, like a couple hundred dollars, and grow it. And so the mindset has to be different because in the past when people graduated from college and began their career, they got to meet with Human Resources, and HR said, "Sign right here, and you can do a match." So you do that, and that's likely the extent of your investment knowledge. Most people never really become wealthy that way. In fact, it wasn't intended for them to become wealthy that way. You really have to look at things like forex, crypto, binary options, e-commerce—things where you can grow your money 1 to 20 percent a day. It's very different from the outdated approaches. And it also gives you access to all of your money as soon as you make it, whereas with the traditional ways—such as bonds and mutual funds—you have to wait for many of those vehicles until you can access your 401k. You have to wait until you retire to have access to the money. However, investing now is so much more.

Buying property, then selling it or renting it out, is a wise investment opportunity that produces streams of income that can lead to great wealth. A while ago, the city of Detroit had properties for sale for $10,000, $20,000, and $30,000. Getting property for $10,000 was *huge!* When you do the math on the purchase of a piece of property for $10,000, you can't deny the wealth potential. For example, say you purchased one property for $10,000 every quarter for one year. At the end of the year, you own four properties. Although you may have to put additional money into them to get them ready for renters, I'm just going to focus on the initial $10,000 to keep this example simple.

So, say you decide to rent the four properties out for $800 per month. For the first year, you will make $9,600 on each property. So, the first year you have made nearly all of your initial investment of $10,000. Now, multiply $9,600 by ten years, and you've made $96,000. Almost $100,000 off of just one $10,000 property. That is huge! For all four properties, the total amount accumulated within a ten-year period would be $384,000. Now, some people may choose to flip and sell the properties for $20,000. However, the money really gets heavy when you rent it out long term.

A few years ago, I sold several properties that I owned to build up some cash flow. I wanted to make some upgrades on other properties that I wanted to rent out. My goal is always to have properties that will provide a stream of income. So, I encourage you to purchase one property a month, two properties a month, or three properties a month. However, don't just think about selling the properties once you get them. Instead, rent them out—because over ten years, that's significant.

You may be wondering, "Why should I buy low-end properties and not high-end properties?" Well, my husband really likes high-end properties more, but I don't because I know I am always going to get my money back with low-end properties. Say, for instance, you spend $200,000 or $400,000 on a high-end property. You rent it out for a good price, but then something happens in the market, and people stop renting. This happened to us a couple of times. People feel pressured when the economy is bad, and they move out of those high-end homes and into homes that cost a lot less. However, the good thing about having homes in the inner city is that they are going to *always* be rented out. But the homes in the suburbs are the first ones to be emptied out.

When you own the lower-cost homes, your profits will always be in the positive. However, if you want to play in the high-end field, just know that it may not necessarily be to your advantage from a return-on-investment standpoint. Maybe it will or maybe it won't. On the other hand, with a lower-income home, you will pretty much always be in the green.

My husband has two rich cousins who are late sixties or early seventies, and they travel all over the world. They are retired schoolteachers, so their pensions aren't really that much. However, they own twenty properties, and each property is paying them approximately $600 to $1,000 per month. So, they have anywhere from $15,000 to $20,000 coming in per month from their properties, which allows them to live very well. It is really a good and empowering feeling to have tenants paying you every month. Although there may be certain costs associated with being a landlord, outside of the monthly rent, have an open line of credit at your bank to help fix repairs—there are expenses in everything. The expenses are big, but the profits should be bigger. Set the price point for rent to offset property expenses—based on market value, location, HOA expenses—per property. If rent is approximately $1,000/mo. with a $20,000 profit, you won't break even until after two years.

You can do that with real estate, oil wells, cryptocurrency, or Bitcoin. If real estate is the route you want to take, set your goals. Do you want to purchase property every month? Do you have a different monthly goal? Or, how many properties do you want to have by the end of the year? While you're still getting income tax refunds, use the money to purchase an income-producing, appreciating asset instead of going shopping or paying a bill. It is better to get an asset that's going to bring you residual income than it is to pay off a bill. Don't get me wrong—I'm all for paying off bills. However, it is vitally important to get money coming in that you don't have to work for.

You may be wondering if you will have to take out a loan every month or if you should use the profit from a sale to buy more properties. Well, you don't have to get a loan every month. You can ask for more money. For instance, if you get approved for $100,000, you may consider asking for $300,000 to buy an apartment building. You can go back to the bank because they are looking for consistency when it comes to your payments. When they see you are making your payments on time, they will usually approve you to receive more money to buy more property. On the other hand, you could take the profit you made on a sale and then buy another property. Either way, I want you to have a long-term vision for your asset accumulation. Here are some other asset accumulation strategies:

- I highly recommend that you get on the link for Quick Silver Start, https://www.quicksilver.me, where you are getting silver every month.

- Oil wells. The way they work is, you can invest in an entire well or a fraction of a well, and then most wells, they drill vertically and horizontally. Most wells pay anywhere between five and twenty years. You can invest in wells by using a reputable oil company—I've shared some on my website, jeweltankard.com—because you have to be careful in the oil industry. They can be a little slick. It costs about $10,000 to purchase one. However, you can begin by setting up an account where you put in $500, then maybe $1,000, and you keep adding to it until you reach the $10,000 needed. I recommend you purchase as many oil wells as you can because you are going to be getting those checks every month for five to twenty years. With Indexed Universal Life Policy (IUL)—a life insurance policy that gives you tax-free retirement and a death benefit—pay a certain amount, and it'll tell you what amount you can get annually tax-free. It pays out monthly/quarterly based off of what you've put into the policy. You will look up one day and realize you've accumulated a lot of cash. You'll be like, "Whoa!"

It is my prayer that you will begin thinking about asset accumulation rather than thinking about simply finding opportunities to buy properties. I want you to have long-range vision and understand that all these things ultimately set you up, so that—when you retire—you will have greater income because you took the money you had coming in and made it work for you.

Not too long ago, I had a conversation with my dad about his mother, who owned ten properties. I thought that was so smart of her to have such a vision in 1980. She was really ahead of her time. I remember that she always had a lot of money. During one of my trips to Georgia, I had the opportunity to visit the house that my dad grew up in and speak with some of the neighbors. It was an emotional moment, and I remember thanking God because, like my grandmother, I have all of this vision and insight. I am walking in it just like she did.

In 2018, I invested in a diamond mine in Liberia. As I waited for my first check to arrive, I made plans to set it aside to prepare to purchase another well or real estate property. I've learned that, when some money comes in, I don't need to be thinking about paying bills. Instead, I may use 50 percent to get out of debt and the other 50 percent to purchase an appreciating asset.

I am passionate about sharing what I know with other women. I want you to live amazing lives. I don't want you to just make money. I don't want you to think short term. Rather, I want you to think long term. I challenge you to decide in your heart and mind to accumulate more assets than you've ever considered before, so that you can live the abundant life that God has empowered you to have. There are new pathways to obtaining wealth, and with hard work and determination, you can become significantly wealthy in a fraction of the time it used to take. Some of those pathways are listed below.

Forex—Foreign Exchange Market

Forex is the largest global financial exchange market, and it's traded twenty-four hours a day, five days a week. Its purpose is to convert one currency into another and trade in foreign currency. Traders can open a forex account and literally buy and sell currencies anywhere in the world. In forex, trading currencies are listed in pairs, and the value is determined relatively by comparing the two currencies in the pair. Profit/loss results in the difference of the price of the currency pair at the time of the transaction.

Pursuing this strategy will create cash flow. Our profit in forex is really powerful. Like I stated above, it's the ability to trade in any two countries with their two currencies, such as the Great Britain Pound (GBP) and Japanese Yen (JPY).

Cryptocurrency

Cryptocurrency is the currency of the future. Crypto is a digital currency that holds value, and it is based on a particular

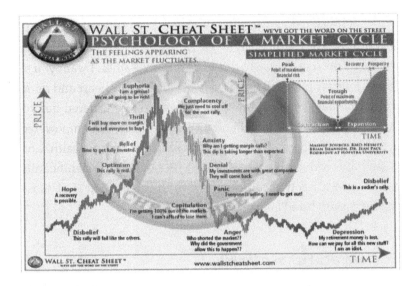

technology. It's used for buying/selling goods and services online. Over nine thousand cryptocurrencies are traded publicly, valued at more than $645 billion. Currently, Bitcoin is the most popular, valued at about $421 billion.

Binary Options

Binary options are transactions where the trader makes a decision that a share in a particular company will go above a certain amount, on a certain date, at a certain time. If the prediction is correct at the time of expiration, the trader has a payout. If the prediction is incorrect, the trader has a loss.

For example, Bobby believes that XYZ, Inc. shares will go above $30 on 2/14/21, at 3:30 pm. As a result, he enters a trade for $100. After the expiration, if the shares go above $30, Bobby has a payout per the agreed terms. However, if the shares don't go above $30, Bobby loses his initial investment.

E-commerce

This is buying/selling of goods using the internet and the transfer of money and data to execute transactions. With e-commerce, you're able to set up a store online and sell products worldwide—it's similar to Amazon. You can set it up with Amazon, and they will do the shipping for you. You can also set up a website, add a payment system (use Amazon), add products, create a FB/IG ad for products, spend $7–$10/day for marketing, and choose a zip code to market in.

Ledger Nano

With new pathways to wealth, there must also be new ways of storing and protecting that wealth. Since cryptocurrency is the new currency, the Ledger Nano wallet is a way to safely store all your digital coins and tokens. It's a hardware wallet that allows safe storage of cryptocurrencies. It also gives you the ability to be able to send and receive different cryptocurrencies.

The financial market is ever evolving and ever changing. You have to position yourself to always be in the know by self-educating and following wealth trends. Everyone leaves clues. You just have to pay attention to the trends, educate yourself, and be willing to trust your financial gut.

JEWEL'S JUMPSTART
· Trust your "knower" (instinct/gut)
· Listen to your heart more than your head
· Trust the first inclination you get

Trusting your financial gut allows you to determine whether you're a producer, a manager, or an investor. A producer is someone who focuses on producing money. A manager is someone who is good at managing money, budgeting, or similar tasks. An investor is very good at multiplying money.

As mentioned previously, not only are crypto and other digital currencies really popular investments, but the real estate market is just as good to capitalize on or invest in. It's income producing. It'll give you money every single month. Again, the goal of the wealthy is to get to a point where you build your interest up so much that it outruns your income, and you could live off of the interest if your income were to stop. Real estate really helps with this because it's residual income. You've got to pay attention because this is an opportunity for you to position yourself to build an empire because you have the education that you need.

Owning real estate is important because you want to have possession of both hard assets and digital assets. A hard asset is anything that comes out of the ground—real estate, gold, silver. Digital assets are cryptocurrencies. Oil wells come out of the ground, so it is considered a hard asset. Having a healthy balance of both is key.

Wealth is definitely attainable, but you have to do research, be willing to learn, and stick with what works best for you. You may already have some things that can be generating income for you, but you may just lack the proper guidance on execution and implementation. That's why I adamantly encourage joining wealth communities. They're able to pull out the best in you—even if you didn't realize it was there.

Millionairess Confession: *I Am Smart!*

Chapter 6

Work Your Income Generators

Income generators are anything that produces income—like e-commerce businesses, trading foreign currency, and even food trucks. It could be anything that produces income on a consistent basis. Since the millionairess is a highly creative, industrious woman who knows how to assert her value in the marketplace, she's well versed in how to work her income generators by seizing opportunities when they're presented. Sometimes, all it takes is a simple conversation to trigger a spark for something more. Having a conversation with someone successful can prompt you to dream bigger and expect more out of life than what you may have been exposed to.

Wealth triggers are basically something that gets you excited and can ultimately produce income. Imagine that you get excited about this thing that you love or are passionate about. It makes you feel good, it's something that you actually like, *and* it can make money for you.

It's like when you hear somebody speak, and it ignites something in you—you realize their destiny could be your destiny. That's what I call wealth triggers: when you see something you've never considered before but are excited about. For example, you might not have been thinking about living in a mansion, but if you walk through the mansions at the Parade of Homes and witness all that beauty, you might think, "Oh my gosh, I must live this way." That's a wealth trigger. Or maybe you get into a Lambo truck, and even though you might not have been thinking about a Lambo, all of a sudden you're like, "This must be mine. I have to have this."

All of those are what I call wealth triggers. You hear somebody. You're exposed to something. You see something that just speaks to the core of your being, something that makes you say, "I need this" or "I'm going to do this." You might walk in an office building one day and say, "I want my own office building. *One day*, I'm going to have my own office building." It's something that then goes into your spirit and snatches it out. After being able to visualize what you want, that mental picture is imbedded within you. Once you're able to visualize what you want, you're then able to manifest it—due to exposure.

And it's usually coupled with joy, excitement—all those things. After being triggered, you have to be ready to move.

To master something, you have to be the student—one that's going to ask questions and be willing to learn. You're have to be an infinite learner. Also, you need to make a decision that you're going to be wealthy. You need to just tell yourself that becoming wealthy is nonnegotiable. The Bible talks about how wealth is a defense—that the wealthy have many friends. And so I need all of you to make a decision right now that becoming wealthy is completely and totally nonnegotiable.

It takes two things to become wealthy. You've got to make the decision, and then you've gotta keep learning. Most people don't make decisive decisions. Most people are indecisive in their life with their money. And so, as a result, they don't ever end up walking into anything because they just won't make the doggone decisions. They don't trust their own instincts.

In 2020, we were really at the beginning stages of the recession—and then Covid-19 began to impact every industry. Some people didn't see it coming because they didn't know the wealth indicators and the wealth cues to look for. But I'm telling you right now, those of you who have been following me and my colleagues and mentors—like Robert and Kim Kiyosaki—I hope you've been paying attention, because this is an opportunity for you to position yourself so that when all of this starts crumbling down, you're still building an empire. You'll have the education that you need so you can make the decisions that you need to make. If you plan ahead economically, you can get the results that you need during every playing point in history.

When you look at what happened during the Great Depression, when you look at what happened during the Great Recession, there were always millionaires and billionaires who came out of those pain points because they had the education and necessary aggression. This is the time for you to take off your passive hat and put on your aggressive hat, so that you can now begin to go into these territories and understand financial markets and make money from them. In 2009, Bitcoin showed up on the scene—for actually one penny. Today, it's over $34,000. It is the fastest growing asset in the entire world. The only reason that we've been building cryptocurrency portfolios is because of this platform. Doing your research is critically, critically important. And this is what I call a wealth indicator.

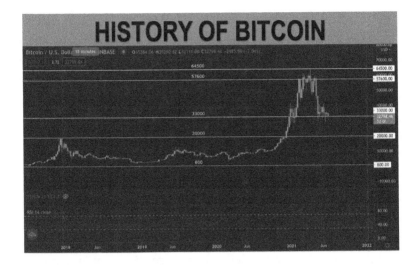

There's an article on Investopedia called, "Cryptocurrency Billionaire Rankings: The Richest People in Crypto," which shows tons of people are becoming billionaires in this cryptocurrency space. I want you to know about this because most people—when they think about becoming wealthy—think it's going to take a long time. But Bitcoin started up in 2009, and now in 2020, people have already become billionaires.

You literally are seeing people become wealthier much faster now than any other time in history. There are a lot of articles out there that I can show you because I want you to know this could be you. But first, you've got to get the education.

Forbes actually has a section that just deals with cryptocurrency. My sister recently sent me a picture of an ATM. She went into the gas station and saw one, and the screen said, "Now taking Bitcoin." I want you to know where we're headed; these are what we call wealth indicators.

Self-Education

You have to tell yourself: "I'm going to become an infinite learner. I want to become a master of money." If you want money, then you're going to have to study it. The reason being that, culturally, we have not necessarily seen a lot of successful people of color holding wealth. That only changes when we start educating ourselves so that we can reap the benefits. You're going to have to have to get continued education.

It's the same thing with wealth. You're going to have to put yourself in a position to be in the flow of wealth—wealth relationships, wealth conversations, wealth strategies. And then what? Then you get wealth results. Dr. Chyna made her first $1M before thirty and developed a community of Digital Entrepreneurs with her online community—Rich University, using forex, cryptocurrency, and e-commerce—once stated it like this during one of our live meetings (edited for length and clarity):

"People are going into stores. Now they're seeing signs talking about preparing for a cashless society—talking about a coin shortage. We're watching banks begin to really buy a lot of Bitcoin. A lot of the uber wealthy are transferring their money from traditional banks and putting it into a cryptocurrency. And we're seeing the shifts now. And I believe that people are starting to kind of wake up. They may not know what's next, but they can obviously see that something's happening right now. You know, we think about the traditional occupations that are no longer needed that are becoming obsolete, and it's really just indicators all around us that there is a digital boom that's taking place right now. I think the biggest thing is that people don't know that they could benefit from it right

now—if they get a position with the right people and just become students of what's happening right now. "It doesn't take you knowing everything. You don't have to have all the answers. You don't even have to have all of the questions to articulate. But what you do have to have is a sense of urgency to move and position right away while you still have access. Because what we're seeing right now is the prices of things that are going to begin to shift. Don't wait for the person who introduced it to you to get to a certain position because that procrastination is going to cost you. It's going to cost you more money when the world is talking about it, and some people are kind of sitting and waiting to see how it's going to pan out. But it's already panning out. "Most millionaires, billionaires, have already been created inside of this space. And now you have an opportunity to get involved, but I don't know that the opportunity will always be here. And when it is—if it is—it's going to definitely cost you a lot more money. So I can't stress enough, Dr. Jewel, the sense of urgency that I believe that everybody needs. And one of the things that I want to say before you go into depth here for women specifically, who may be wearing a lot of hats and who may be taking care of your families and in school and working, taking care of your spouse, your parents, and all of those things, you need to understand that 15 to 20 minutes a day could absolutely change your life. It's not you having to learn every intricate detail about this to become profitable. We have systems already in place that allow you to literally copy and paste the experts so that you are not left behind. This is the ringing of the bell. This is the writing on the wall. This is us alerting you now to really move aggressively and get in position."

When you sign up, you are basically saying: "Listen, I'm ready to educate myself. I'm ready to learn." So one of the first things that's gonna happen is, you're gonna have tons of support. You're going to be connected to us. You're going to be connected to a whole support team. And I'm going to tell you right now, that's been a real blessing in this space—realizing that it's not just me in here trying to figure it out. There's no way I would've become a good trader on my own.

Getting the self-education puts all this access at your fingertips. Mainly in the beginning, because you're copying and pasting which pairs to trade with the technology and many of the tools that allow you to feel competent. Not because you know everything, but because you've been able to grow your demo account, and you are consistent with it. So, practicing trading fifteen to thirty minutes a day can be life changing for a lot of people.

Millionairess Confession: *I Am Anointed!*

Chapter 7

Decrease So You Can Increase

Reducing debt and compulsive, impulsive spending are practical ways for you to get your money going in the right direction. So much about building wealth is developing discipline and learning proper stewardship. Most of us are raised to spend money on what we want, with no thought to the future or the repercussions of that spending. I really want every woman to have what she desires, what she needs...but she's also gonna have to learn that some of these things aren't going to happen immediately or all at once. There are other goals that may need to be achieved before we just really started splurging. For example, if you know you're making under $10–15,000 a month, I will probably tell you to go ahead and cut the cable. You really don't need to be watching entertainment right now till you get yourself in a base price.

You have to look at your spending. Some people will go to the mall every single month and go shopping for shoes and clothes.

You might say, "Okay, you know what, normally I would go and spend on average of $300 to $1,000 every time I go to the mall. For the next quarter, I'm not going to do that. I'm going to actually start putting that money in investing." That's why financial journaling is really important because sometimes we don't really realize where our money is going.

When you put it down on paper, you'll say, "Oh, I do spend a lot of money on purses or bags or clothes." I love those things too, and I want every girl to have as many as she wants—but we gotta make sure we're handling our money and getting the disciplines of wealth down first. Then we can move over to some of the fun stuff. I would say Netflix/Hulu and other streaming services, possibly even travel, should be put on hold for a season. Even though I definitely want all my girls to travel—because exposure is key to knowing what's out there—you might have to say, "Okay, this year, we're not going to really do the travel that we normally do. I'm going to put that money in investing." When you see it, you can start believing you can have it.

I'm more concerned with money being properly invested than I am with you just paying off debt. When you pay off debt, it's important it's not growing you or your money forward. Let's just say you have a $1,000 Visa. Once you pay off that $1,000, you're never gonna see that money again. But if I invest $1,000 in the right place, that $1,000 can turn into $5,000. My concern first and foremost is always going to be for you to invest heavily and *then* pay off debt. For example, here's a true story: I have a credit card that I use for my real estate investing. I have $20,000 on my card right now. Well, I have a check that's going to be coming in for about $25,000. So the way that's going to be broken up and spent is, I'll pay my tithe and offering—a $2,000 tithe and a $1,000 offering. I will invest $20,000 and then take $2,000 and pay off the card. Now, most people might take the entire $20,000 and pay off the card. Not me. I'm going to take it and invest it because I can turn that $20,000 into six-figures within a couple of months. So, what makes more sense in the long run?

There is a difference between good debt and bad debt. Bad debt would be a car note. Good debt would be anything that you have acquired to get an asset. Let's say you found an apartment building that you want to buy, and it's $100,000. So you get that apartment building for $100,000, but that apartment building is going to bring you, let's just say, $10,000–$15,000 a month. Well, that's considered good debt because anything that is going to actually create income for you is good debt. Anything that does not create an income for you is bad debt. For example, buying a house is not an asset unless it's creating cashflow.

A lot of times people think their house is an asset, but it's not. Your house is actually a liability. Now, if you sell it and get profit from it, then it's an asset, and you can profit off it that way. But as long as you're living in that house, that house is a liability. Once it's sold, then it turns into whatever profit you make—if indeed, profit can be made.

Credit Cards

I think credit cards are good, but only if they're spent on the right things. You should use credit cards for the purpose of business credit and personal credit. Ultimately, all of your purchases in terms of assets will ideally reach a point where you're using your business name to purchase those assets. Sometimes, people say, "I don't need credit cards because I'll just use them." That's why you've got to create a discipline for yourself. Tell yourself, "Okay, this credit card is not spent for this." Personally, I like American

Express in particular because you can get points and travel and other benefits like that. I recommend everybody having American Express. They'll also help you to categorize all your spending. I really like American Express because that tool is helpful for a business owner. I really recommend you having it in your business name and not necessarily your personal name. The idea is to move as much as possible out of your personal name and into your business. It's better to have business credit cards than personal credit cards.

Credit cards, ideally, should not be used to live off of. Unfortunately, sometimes when people are not making enough income, they do live off of it. They use credit cards to buy their groceries. Now, it's one thing if you use the credit card to buy your groceries, but you have the cash that you can use, and you're just using the credit card to earn points and other rewards. In all actuality, the last thing you should want to do is spend money to buy groceries with a credit card—unless, like I said, there are some type of rewards involved. Again, that's why I like American Express. They don't charge you all that interest as long as you pay the balance within thirty days. But with normal credit cards, you've got all that interest. You spent $150 at the grocery store, but by the time you pay the card off, its's really $200. You need to pay attention to the interest rate that you are paying.

Overall, it's better to have business credit cards. If you currently have personal credit cards, I would close them out and not use them anymore. I would instead try to establish an LLC and open up an American Express business card with that LLC. Let's just say, for example, your credit is not good; if so, then you might have to hold on to it and not close it. You can visit http://novaemoneyfunding.com for further assistance with your credit because in the end, you need to get your business and your personal credit together.

Jewel's Gem

Credit cards, ideally, should not be used to live off of.

You may have to cut back on your spending and splurging for a while. For instance, I never buy a new car. I buy pre-owned, and I'll take the car that I have, and then I will sell it for another pre-owned car. Then I pay the difference in cash. That way, I don't have any debt on it. I do that every time I get a new car. Brand new cars, as soon as you drive them off the lot...well, the depreciation is ridiculous. Also, make sure you're getting the oil changed regularly and keeping your car well maintained. Then you don't have to worry about, "Oh my gosh, my car is breaking down on me," because you weren't taking care of it.

You need to get your credit up because bad credit impacts all your insurances...your car insurance, your homeowners insurance, even your life insurance. So, having good credit is super, super important. That should be a number one priority—getting that credit together. Which means sitting down and calling all those creditors and working it out. If it's been over seven years, the company on the link provided will help you with getting it off of your credit all together. That'll raise the score, which then makes you eligible for lower-cost insurances.

Most companies don't tell you that, but that's the truth. Bad credit and higher interest equals higher car insurance, homeowners insurance, and life insurance. Also, it's important to note that if you have an eviction on your file, you should try to work it out with the landlord. That eviction makes it very hard to rent or purchase, but they can take it off your credit.

Medical Bills

The same thing applies to your old medical bills. A lot of times, financial aid is available for old medical bills. Go ahead and call the hospital and say, "Hey, this bill is outstanding. I know I owe this. It's going to go to collections soon, but I want to work something out. I've got this huge bill, but I can't afford it. Do you guys have any kind of financial aid that I can apply for to help me pay this bill?" Hospitals have what they call angel investors. They have all kinds of stuff for medical bills.

So if you have past medical bills, call the hospital and ask for the financial aid department. They'll usually send you some paperwork to fill out. It's not a loan; once it's paid, you're good. I usually do that at the end of the year, though lately, things have quieted down. But in the past, I would call the insurance companies and then the city office. Insurance companies are always adding on new features that can help you receive a discounted rate.

Incidentals

I also want you to really look at your homeowners insurance and call your homeowners company. Whether you're renting and have renter's insurance or you own your home, you should call your insurance agency. A lot of times, they can reduce your rate. Let's just say that it's a year where the taxes go down, or you believe the taxes have gone down. A lot of times, they're not going to automatically lower your property taxes; however, if you call them and say, "Hey, I believe that I'm due for a reduction on my property taxes," you might see results.

We've actually reduced our taxes by a couple thousand dollars a year just because we called. When they looked at it, they were like, "Oh, actually, we can reduce." For example, houses were really inflated in '03, '04, and '05. When that recession came in '07 and '08, all the property taxes were reduced. And everybody was losing, and prices of houses came down. They reduced people's property taxes for the ones that called. Even with your home-owners insurance, you can say, "Hey, I want to see if anything can be done."

Run a comparison. If you have several homes together or if you have a couple cars, see if you can get the multi-discount. Double-check to make sure that stuff is added. Sometimes, you think it's added, but that's not necessarily the case. Call your homeowners insurance. Call and see if you can get it reduced. Call down to the city to see if they'll reduce your property taxes. Call homeowners, property taxes, cable—really, almost anything. Even if you have credit card debt, you can call and say, "I want to know if I can reduce my credit card interest rates." You can call them and ask them that. All those questions are really important. A lot of times, everything can be reduced with just a phone call.

Cash, Credit, or Debit?

When budgeting, you should get in the habit of spending cash and not using a debit or credit card all the time. Pull out the amount that you need for cash, and once you spend that, you don't use your card. This allows you to discipline your spending habits. Once you've spent the allotted cash, you are done spending for the week, and you can't use your debit card to continue spending. Also, you should put a couple hundred dollars in your wallet and tell yourself you can't spend it because you have to get used to keeping money on you. With a lot of people, whenever they get money, they spend it all. But not a millionairess. You've got to get used to having money on you, so that you get out of that "I'm broke until Friday" scenario. You've got to get used to keeping money on you all the time and then come up with a fixed amount of what you need and pursue it.

Jewel's Gem

I always buy pre-owned cars!

Cooking or Eating Out?

Cooking at home makes a difference. Not only is it budget friendly, but it's a lot healthier. I literally just washed a whole chicken, cut up some onions and garlic, and just stuck in the oven. My husband and I eat out, but we don't eat out every night, though not necessarily so much for financial reasons right now. Eating in allows you to make meals according to your dietary needs, like low-sodium or low-sugar diets. Overall, it's a lot healthier to eat at home and definitely a lot more cost effective.

I definitely want everybody to be at a point where if they want it, they can get it. You just have to be able to know that maybe it's not the right time to get it, and that happens at every level. One person may really want a Fendi bag, while someone else might want a new Tesla. At either point, you've got to know if it's time for you to do this or not.

More than likely, your income is not going to increase unless you get some self-education. You can pursue higher education, but that's not the times we're in right now. I know people with master's degrees and PhDs who still aren't multimillionaires because it's just a different time. If you want to increase your income, you are going to have to increase your knowledge. You've got to get wealthy mentors to show you how to do it.

Otherwise, it'll always be too tight, always be paycheck to paycheck. You'll always be looking for a raise, even though a raise on a job is not really helpful—if they give you a 10–20 percent raise but inflation went up 10–20 percent, did you really get an increase? I don't think so. That's why most people, when they get raises, don't see a change in their lifestyles.

In the end, purses, shoes, and cars—though they are nice, and I am a girl who likes nice things—will never affirm you as well as building your own financial legacy. Unless the designer item has your name on it, you are not building your financial legacy, your financial wealth, or your financial pie...which we'll discuss in the next chapter.

Millionairess Confession: *I Am a Great Investor!*

Chapter 8

Create Your Financial Pie

In this chapter, you will receive practical information on what a millionairess's holdings should look like. The graphs and tables within these pages will allow you to see exactly where your money should be going. Your financial pie will include investments that are good to acquire, which will ultimately help position you for becoming the millionairess you're destined to be. There are many flavors of pies, so it stands to reason that there are many types of financial pies. In the paragraphs below, I'll be offering insights on some investments that are working really well for me. For example, as I said in Chapter 5, I personally feel that the first slice of your pie needs to be 40 percent cryptocurrency. Bitcoin, in 2009, was one penny; today, it's right at about $43,000 with speculation of it getting to $650,000, $1 million, $1.5 million—that's where it's headed. As a result, we need to make sure that you are heavily invested in crypto. It is, after all, the future of money.

After the 40 percent investment in crypto, the next slice you need to add to your pie is 20 percent in tech and innovation stock. Both of these types of stocks are performing very well in

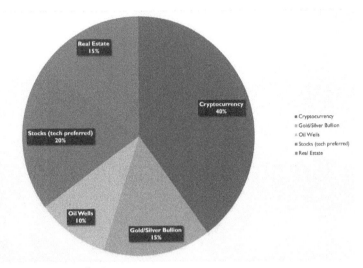

CHART 1. Financial Pie

investment markets. New, innovative, and cutting-edge stocks usually always perform well in the market.

The next slice is 15 percent in gold/silver bullion, specifically, and not the paper stock. Bullion is actual coins, bars, and rounds, which have been produced from mints and precious metal refiners.

Your next pie slice should be 15 percent in real estate. As I stated in Chapter 5, investing in real estate can be very lucrative. A primary way to make money in real estate is by becoming a landlord of a rental property. Flipping properties can bring in quite a bit of income as well.

Lastly, your pie needs a 10 percent investment in oil wells. Investing in oil wells can be financially beneficial, but it can also carry an equal amount of risks. Be sure you use a reputable company. After drilling, oil wells can produce for twenty to forty years. Can you imagine getting residual income from one investment for several decades? That's why self-education is so important. Most people don't know about this kind of stuff, but now that you're on your way to becoming a millionairess, *you* do.

Diversification

Diversification is essentially mixing a wide variety of investments into your portfolio. Other than what's already listed on the financial pie, I don't think it should be too diversified, though. I think you need to pick an industry and stick with it. I really prefer tech stocks—opportunities that deal with the future. You know what I mean—Tesla, Amazon, Apple, Silicon Valley, Google. Even medical research for vaccinations—like for Covid-19—and other rare things that will come out from companies like Pfizer: some of the top-notch, innovative technology in the medical industry.

I also recommend real estate buying and holding and putting in tenants, so I have that residual income coming in all the time. For immediate cash, a buy and flip is good.

Overall, though, I'm not so big on diversification. I'm not really one to meander off and just be investing. I think you should focus on hard or digital assets. There are tons of things to invest in, but it's just like with cryptocurrency, for example—you don't need to buy all crypto. Not *all* crypto is going to have the sustainability and longevity. But there are certainly some main cryptos that I think are imperative to have: Bitcoin, Ethereum, Litecoin, and Ripple. In my opinion, those are the main cryptos that every millionairess needs to have. You can get more info by enrolling in Mastery Academy (imarketslive.com).

Jewel's Gem 💎

For immediate cash, a buy and flip is good.

Compound Interest

Compound interest is basically interest on top of interest. Anything that you do over time will cause exponential growth. It's reinvesting interest instead of having it paid out. By doing so, the next period's interest is earned on the principal sum, plus previously accumulated interest.

You can also download the compound interest calculator for help in calculating compound interest.

Compound interest is the ability to grow your money significantly by using the right financial investment instruments. For example, I could start an account with $200 and grow it to $20,000 in thirty to sixty days by trading foreign currency/cryptocurrency. You always want to invest your money in things that have the ability to compound your money. For example, old financial tools like CDs, bonds, and mutual funds had compounded interest, but it was very slow. They paid out anywhere from 1 percent to maybe 8 percent a year. That used to be considered good—you got 8 percent a year on your money. Now, with the new rules of money, you can grow your money 1 percent to 8 percent per day.

I Got My Lump Sum

When you get a large sum of money at once, that's not your time to "live large and in charge." Firstly, you should pay your tithe and offering, and then you should pay yourself. I recommend paying

Compound Interest Chart: 30 Days

Day	Date	Earnings	Reinvest	(Principal/Cash Out)	TOTAL Principal	TOTAL Cash
1	Fri Jul 09 2021	16.00	100%	(16.00/0.00)	216.00	0.00
2	Mon Jul 12 2021	17.28	100%	(17.28/0.00)	233.28	0.00
3	Tue Jul 13 2021	18.66	100%	(18.66/0.00)	251.94	0.00
4	Wed Jul 14 2021	20.16	100%	(20.16/0.00)	272.10	0.00
5	Thu Jul 15 2021	21.77	100%	(21.77/0.00)	293.87	0.00
6	Fri Jul 16 2021	23.51	100%	(23.51/0.00)	317.38	0.00
7	Mon Jul 19 2021	25.39	100%	(25.39/0.00)	342.77	0.00
8	Tue Jul 20 2021	27.42	100%	(27.42/0.00)	370.19	0.00
9	Wed Jul 21 2021	29.62	100%	(29.62/0.00)	399.81	0.00
10	Thu Jul 22 2021	31.98	100%	(31.98/0.00)	431.79	0.00
11	Fri Jul 23 2021	34.54	100%	(34.54/0.00)	466.33	0.00
12	Mon Jul 26 2021	37.31	100%	(37.31/0.00)	503.64	0.00
13	Tue Jul 27 2021	40.29	100%	(40.29/0.00)	543.93	0.00
14	Wed Jul 28 2021	43.51	100%	(43.51/0.00)	587.44	0.00
15	Thu Jul 29 2021	47.00	100%	(47.00/0.00)	634.44	0.00
16	Fri Jul 30 2021	50.76	100%	(50.76/0.00)	685.20	0.00
17	Mon Aug 02 2021	54.82	100%	(54.82/0.00)	740.02	0.00
18	Tue Aug 03 2021	59.20	100%	(59.20/0.00)	799.22	0.00
19	Wed Aug 04 2021	63.94	100%	(63.94/0.00)	863.16	0.00
20	Thu Aug 05 2021	69.05	100%	(69.05/0.00)	932.21	0.00
21	Fri Aug 06 2021	74.58	100%	(74.58/0.00)	1006.79	0.00
22	Mon Aug 09 2021	80.54	100%	(80.54/0.00)	1087.33	0.00
23	Tue Aug 10 2021	86.99	100%	(86.99/0.00)	1174.32	0.00
24	Wed Aug 11 2021	93.95	100%	(93.95/0.00)	1268.27	0.00
25	Thu Aug 12 2021	101.46	100%	(101.46/0.00)	1369.73	0.00
26	Fri Aug 13 2021	109.58	100%	(109.58/0.00)	1479.31	0.00
27	Mon Aug 16 2021	118.34	100%	(118.34/0.00)	1597.65	0.00
28	Tue Aug 17 2021	127.81	100%	(127.81/0.00)	1725.46	0.00
29	Wed Aug 18 2021	138.04	100%	(138.04/0.00)	1863.50	0.00
30	Thu Aug 19 2021	149.08	100%	(149.08/0.00)	2012.58	0.00

yourself in cryptocurrency and/or gold or silver. Visit Quick Silver (https://quicksilver.me/), where you can invest in gold and silver. When I say pay yourself in gold or silver, that means you purchase it, and they'll ship it to you. Again, after you pay your tithe and offering and you pay yourself, *then* you can go ahead and pay your bills. Gold and silver are hard assets (anything that comes out of the ground) that gain more value over time. Advantage—it's an inflation hedge against the dollar—can be used to purchase real estate.

It's really important to use autosave too. In building wealth, you want to get consistent. By using autosave, your information is automatically saved, and transactions can be made more effortlessly. You don't want to just hit a link.

Appreciating Assets

An appreciating asset is anything that will gain value over time. Conversely, depreciating assets are anything that will lose value over time. Appreciating assets contribute to your financial pie because the more appreciating assets you have, the more your wealth is growing. For example, if I buy silver at $10, and then buy some wells for $10, and the price for both goes up to $700, my portfolio has just grown. If I buy gold at $1,000, but then it grows to $3,000, then I just had a $2,000 profit on every ounce that I own. As the value of the dollar goes down, the value of gold goes up. If I cash it in, then I'll see a profit or I could take the gold or silver.

What most people don't know is that you can take most assets and make purchases with other assets. So, let's just say, for example, you have the equivalent of $10,000 of gold, and all of a sudden, some gold you bought for $10,000 about ten years ago is now worth $300,000. Let's say you take that gold and purchase a $300,000 house. You could possibly negotiate with the owner of that house to purchase that house with gold—or purchase that house with silver or Bitcoin. People are actually buying real estate with Bitcoin. This is beneficial because you'll need a lot less gold, silver, or Bitcoin to purchase real estate than you would need cash.

Millionairess Confession: *I Am a Great Strategist!*

Chapter 9

Appoint Your
Financial Cabinet

By simply building relationships and networking with people, you're going to grow. The top five people who you're closest to—if you look at how much money they make or how much money they're worth, that's probably what you're going to be worth. If the top five people in your circle are making under $100,000 a year, more than likely, that's what you're going to make. If the top five people in your life are making $5 million a year, then that's probably what you're going to make. So, relationships become extremely vital. You can only grow from what you've been exposed to. It becomes really important that you purposefully connect yourself with other people who are smarter than you so you can keep growing. It's impossible to grow if you don't get the information. If you don't put yourself in a position where you start learning what's happening and then implementing what you're learning, then you have no growth.

Most adults live the same life over and over again. That's why you can go to Uncle Bubba's house and see he's got that same couch, with that same TV, with that same blanket, with that same pillow, with that same comforter on his bed. He probably has not put himself in a position to be around other people who say, "You know, it's time to throw that couch out and get a new couch. It's time to get a new kitchen counter. It's time to get a new *anything*." How you live and your quality of life is determined by what you see and what you hear all the time. It's extremely important for you to network, so you can grow past your world today.

Wealth Mentor

If you don't have a wealth mentor, you're not going to be able to grow past what you're not exposed to. If you're at a point where nobody is giving you any kind of instruction, and that's really for anything—that's money, that's marriage, that's family—then you need to seek out mentorship. Maybe you're strong in money, but your family is torn apart; in this case, maybe you need a mentor to tell you, "Hey, you need to set aside family vacations," or, "Hey, is it time you had a family meeting?" or, "Hey, when was the last time you asked your children what else they need from you?" Or even, "When was the last time you went to church?" or, "When was the last time you opened up your Bible and read it?" If we desire to grow in any particular area, then all of us need mentorship in every area of life.

Without mentorship, a lot of times, we just forget what's available to us. So, it's not that you don't want to grow—you just forget that you need help. You need to be reminded. Maybe you need to be reminded of this or you need to be reminded of that. Those things become really important. And like I said, that's for every area. We're not just talking about wealth but also how you can have a successful marriage, for example, and still be a boss babe.

There's an art to that. Sometimes, women don't know how to handle this stuff, and they become dominant and mean. But that's not necessary. You can still embrace your femininity. You don't have to go crazy just because you got some bags. You can still be nice to people. Ideally, when it comes to mentorship, you'll get a mentor for every area of your life so that *every* area continues to grow. Otherwise, if you don't spend time and effort on it, then that part of your life is not going to get better.

It's just like the effort you put into your family. Maybe when Big Mama was alive, everybody got together a lot because Big Mama cultivated and fostered everybody coming over on Sundays, or everybody coming over on this day or that holiday. And so that created a strong family unit. But then Big Mama dies, and nobody's making plans anymore. What happened? You think, *We used to get together*. But nobody took on leadership in that area to serve as a mentor for your family members.

Jewel's Gem

You can still embrace your femininity.

Having a Relationship with a CPA

As a millionairess, you want to make sure your taxes are in order. Maybe when you weren't making that much money, you could go down the street to H&R Block. But as your money starts multiplying, you need someone who is savvier—who understands tax advantages, legal tax advantages, legal tax avoidance, how to properly use a business trust, how to establish a family trust, or how to file for a foundation. Maybe you're not there yet, but you still want to get most of your business expenses written off. If your money is not being handled right, you can end up owing Uncle Sam a whole lot of money. You are making the money, but you had nobody to actually put in order. Remember, keeping things in order at every level is extremely important.

Having a Relationship with an Attorney

Things are going to come up. There's going to be people out there who try to take advantage of you or pull one over on you because they know you've achieved a level of success. You're going to have to have an attorney help you at every stage: not just before you do the deal, but maybe in the middle of the deal and at the end of the deal. You need to have someone you trust, someone who is not trying to just bill you every time you make a phone call. You respect their time, but also realize it's a long-standing business relationship.

If I have a question, I need to be able to get on the phone and call my attorney. I've learned that, being in reality TV, I have to have an entertainment attorney. But then if something happened in my business, my entertainment attorney couldn't necessarily help me. I needed a business attorney as well. And if something ever goes on with my taxes, I may need a tax attorney. So as you grow, you're going to have to possibly employ or connect with attorneys who are specialists in particular areas.

Having a Relationship with a Certified Financial Planner

I don't think really having a relationship with a certified financial planner is as important as doing your own self-education. Because the reality is that they, a lot of times, are going after what we call the "old rules of money." They're going to try and push you toward mutual funds, CDs, and bonds—things like that. I don't think that's as important. I think self-education and getting in a wealth group and a wealth community is going to be a lot more advantageous. Nobody becomes wealthy off of those strategies, at least not quickly.

Building a Financial Cabinet of Advisors

Joining organizations like The Millionairess Club is really important because it's putting you in a position to meet other women and experts in the money flow. You're going to build through joining clubs like that, and other clubs like it are also going to be really important. Make it a priority to go to their events as well. In person, you'll be able to know if this is someone you want to connect with or not.

For a lot of women, the people you're looking to grow from won't always have your same beliefs. Some of them are going to have foul mouths. Some of them might be atheists, but they may be geniuses in their particular skillsets. So I would definitely say that you're in the relationship not to get fed spiritually but to build your wealth account. And that becomes really important because I've seen a lot of people miss out on relationships because they were like, "Such and such is not saved or doesn't believe in God." You need to see it like this: *I want you to believe in God, but I don't need that for you to be what you are in my life. You are here to help me build wealth. I understand that you are here to help me build wealth. And so I'm not here to judge your walk.* Hopefully, your life can impact them in some way. But that's not necessary for you to have a wealth-building relationship with them.

Jewel's Gem 💎

I want you to believe in God,
but I don't need that for what you are in my life.

Minding My Business

Although some people may be living the reverse of how I live, it's really not my business how they're living their life if they're adding value to my wealth portfolio. Think about it—when you go to the gas station, you don't look at the guy who's pumping your gas or the owner of the gas station and decide on pumping or not pumping your gas there, depending on their beliefs. As a customer, you don't care. You get the gas, and you go on about your business. That does not matter to you.

When you go into the grocery store, you're not like, "Okay, I need to talk to the owner. I need to know what he believes before I buy his food." No, you go in there and you buy the food—period! You don't even think about it 'cause you don't care. You went to the grocery store and got what you went for, which was food. You do not care about who the checkout girl is spending her time with. You don't care about what she does outside of work. All you know is you came, you paid your money, you got your food, and now your family is straight.

We have to do the same thing in business. We can't try to police people's lives, especially not when they could possibly take us to the million flow. It doesn't mean we're going to do business with every person, nor am I saying that I do business with every wicked person. What I am saying is that, if I've identified a particular genius in someone, I'm going to stay open to letting them teach me and not get into the business of judging their lives. I'm never going to be one of those people constantly saying, "I ain't doing business with that person." If you do, when you look up, all the people you got in your circle will be saved but broke; thus, you'll stay saved and broke. Hopefully, with my approach, I can influence their lives because they also see my life. That's the whole goal. I can pattern their principles without necessarily patterning their lifestyle.

Team Building

I really look forward to meetings with my team. We get together in a room and work hard to come up with ideas that will keep the brand relevant. Sometimes, it's just getting together and saying, "What do we need to do to tweak this? What do we need to do to add this?" I believe we have to keep thinking about ways to improve. I realize that I can't do everything; therefore, I rely on the skillsets of my team members. Allowing my team members to walk in their genius and assist me with my ideas is huge.

If you have a business and your team isn't supporting you in a positive manner, you may be hesitant to fully trust working with them. Instead, you may be inclined to be in the trenches alone. However, I think that is very dangerous. We have all had disappointments, betrayals, or dealings with jealousy or envy—but it is best not to focus on that. If you are dealing with trust issues, I suggest you meditate on Philippians 3:13. Paul warns the church to really forget those things that are behind them. Instead, we must spend more time creating our future. You are going to have to press on. More importantly, you have to overcome the fear of thinking, "What if I get hurt again?"

I suffered all kinds of abuse when I was married to my first husband. In those moments when I was being abused or hurt, I could have easily decided never to trust another man again. But I had to take responsibility for the part I played. Nobody made me marry him. That was my choice, and the person I was then and the one I have become now are very different.

So in every instance where you feel like you've been betrayed or had to deal with someone's jealousy, be sure to take responsibility, and think back to see if there were warning signs that you ignored. Because there are always warning signs. There were plenty of them in my relationship with my first husband, but I kept ignoring them. I thought if I just prayed about it, or if I just did this or that, things would get better. Please don't ignore the warning signs!

When it comes to working with a team, it's important to remember that no man is an island. God doesn't want you trying to do everything on your own. As a matter of fact, God created the first team (or partnership), Adam and Eve. He told them to be fruitful and multiply because He didn't call them to be on this earth by themselves. Everyone else was born from Adam and Eve, who had children, and their children had children. All through the Bible, there are stories about people in partnership, such as Jesus and His twelve disciples; Esther and Mordecai; Jonathan and David; Paul and Silas; and Aquila and Priscilla. Everything throughout the Word goes back to a partnership, a collaboration. So, if God did that, so can I.

Every day, I give positive confessions over the team. I confess that they are highly paid—six or seven figure earners—and that they are brilliant, supernatural thinkers. I believe whatever I meditate on daily is what I am going to become, and that also applies to the people around me. I attract what I've been constantly thinking.

So, I think writing down your confessions and speaking them over yourself and your team every day will be very beneficial in creating a great and powerful working relationship. Remember, your thinking causes thoughts, and your thoughts cause words, and your words cause actions and behaviors. Eventually, your whole lifestyle is made from what you think and say.

When I'm looking for team members, I definitely look for people who have a certain level of confidence with a particular genius—because I know one genius will beget another. I also look for good people, and people who are honest. And last but not least, I like to work with happy people. Not people who are easily offended, hurt all the time, and always have drama. When I come to work, I want to create, not counsel. I want people to come to work whole. I realize everyone goes through seasons, and that's fine, but I'm talking about people who always have an issue. I want to work with good people who are grounded. At the very least, I want people who like people and are willing to add value to others. I want them to feel good about themselves and others and not focus on other people's flaws. Instead, I want them to focus on other people's geniuses.

Jewel's Gem

I know one genius will beget another.

There are some people I work with who make other people ask, "Why are you working with them?" I answer, "I work with them because I found their genius." I work with that genius, and hopefully over time, I can demonstrate well enough what things should look like and have a positive influence on them. I am not going to throw people away because I've identified a flaw or a weakness. I wouldn't want people doing that to me. Also, I watch how I think about people because every thought is a seed that I'm sowing. So, if I'm sowing good thoughts then I set myself up to harvest a lot of that back. Regardless of whether or not I work with them closely or from a distance, I try to make sure that my thoughts and words about people are good. Yes, it is something I have to work on. It's not automatic.

I don't necessarily look for people who have the same beliefs as I do. From a business standpoint, I don't believe that has to be a requirement. Even if they are an atheist, hopefully, my life will make a positive impact on them. So although I want them to love my God, they don't have to. I just pray that my life will make them want to love Him. My main concern is that they are good at what they do and ready to do business.

Camille Westmoreland, COO of the Jewel Tankard Brand, shared some valuable information on building a super team with our members of The Millionairess Club. Here's what she said:

"As an entrepreneur, you are the visionary of the thing you are trying to bring to pass. Therefore, there are certain qualities you must possess so that your team will actually want to stay around you. Otherwise, you will find yourself constantly having to replace people.

"So, who needs a team? You do. Whether you have a brick-and-mortar business or an online business, the reality is, you can't do everything. One type of business may need a larger team than another, but still, you cannot be an island. In order to keep going from one level to the next, you need other people in place to help you get there.

"Why is the team important? Many times, Dr. Jewel will have an idea and throw it out to her team, so we can all come

together and hash it out. Together, we figure out how that idea can grow. However, if she had kept the idea to herself, without someone to bounce it off of, it could have only gone so far.

"As a leader, you must realize that you don't have to know everything. I recently saw a quote on Facebook that said, 'You don't have to have a degree to start your own business, but to work for a boss, you have to have a degree.' To me, that simply means that companies believe people with degrees know more, so they put them in positions to help push the vision. And that is the same mentality you want to have. It is okay to have people connected to you who are smarter than you. The only thing that really matters is that you are securing the bag. I've seen this mentality in Dr. Jewel, and it has flowed down to us as we operate our own businesses.

"Having a team also allows you to leverage skills beyond your own. So, if you are a producer, there are activities you do to generate high income. There are other activities you do that are low-dollar or no-dollar activities. Having a team allows you to put people in place to take care of those things that don't really bring in that big income. In a nutshell, your time should be focused on income-producing activity. That's the key. So think about the tasks you have to accomplish that are not producing income, and those are the ones you want to delegate to your team.

"Another reason having a team is so important is that it removes you from being a bottleneck, which is a person who does everything, causing a decrease in productivity. You can't grow beyond yourself if you're doing everything. Author John Maxwell calls this 'the law of the lid.' You become the lid that is preventing your own growth. However, with a team, you can get beyond that lid or ceiling.

"I connected with Dr. Jewel in September of 2011. I am originally from Winston-Salem, North Carolina, and my home church was in the process of dissolving at the time. I was twenty-nine years old and had lived in the same city my entire life. I asked God for direction and what to do next. Dr. Jewel invited me to a church in Murfreesboro, Tennessee, for a business meeting. While there, I met two women (Marquita and Yasheia). I loved their church, and from September to March, I drove seven to eight hours twice a month to attend church there. Eventually, I moved to Murfreesboro, got a job, and started serving in the ministry there.

"Dr. Jewel had her Millionairess Club, and they were doing meetings at our church in Murfreesboro. The reach was really only to people in the middle Tennessee area, but when she would travel, she had all of these people wanting to connect with her. At the time, I was just participating, and I was getting ideas about things that would be great for her Millionairess Club. Finally, in 2015, I said, 'You know, Dr. Jewel, we have to take this to the next level.'

"I became a personal assistant to Dr. Jewel in 2015. We began to make some changes to the way things had been previously done and created the online Millionairess Club so we could reach more people. We began to get over two hundred people plugging in on a consistent basis.

"Our goal is to get thousands and thousands of people, and we are constantly implementing new strategies to reach that goal. However, what would have happened if Dr. Jewel wasn't open to having a team, and she wanted to do everything herself? Most likely, her outreach would have remained the same, with very little growth.

"Now, I am sure you have experienced burnout at some point in your life. I know I have. Burnout is sure to occur when you're doing everything. It's doing the things you hate to do, but they must be done. A team will help you get rid of the tasks you don't like to do, which will ultimately prevent you from experiencing burnout. I look for interns and assistants to do the things I don't want to do. I also value their perspectives. Although I have my own thought process, I allow my team to help me bring full shape and form to it. I don't see my team as 'I'm the boss, and they're my team.' We are a team. So, I challenge you to be open to the perspectives of your team members and allow them to help you develop and grow your vision. Give them space to create and use their God-given abilities to help advance your brand. Another point I want to make is, when you work on your own, you are only challenged to the extent that you can muster your own motivation and discipline. Having a qualified team will further challenge you because the team will expect your best and will push you to be your best. Here are some specific qualities you should look for when putting your team together:

- Make sure the people you choose are passionate about what they do.
- Are they intrinsically motivated or money motivated? You do not want someone on your team who's solely motivated by the paycheck. While money is a great motivator, you won't get the best out of that person. You want people who love what they do and see value in what you do.
- Is the person committed to mastery? In other words, is she looking to be better?

- *Is the individual reliable?*
- *Is she honest?*
- *Does the person have a positive attitude?*
- *Does the individual think ahead?*
- *Will she own your vision?*
- *Is the person flexible?*
- *Is the person team-focused?*

"Now, as a leader, here are some of the qualities you do not want to possess:

"Being a micromanager. You don't want the people on your team to feel as though you don't trust them to do their jobs. Instead, be a macro-manager: someone who gives the directives and allows the team to carry them out. You don't have to stand over those on your team to make sure things are getting done. You just want to see the end results. I'm not saying you shouldn't check on things, but your main focus should be on the bigger goals, not all the minute tasks.

"Lacking vision. You must have a vision or a goal so your team can take you where you are trying to go. Make sure your vision is clear, and your team is aware of it. Put it out there, and let them help you bring it to pass.

"Lacking adaptability. Never be the kind of leader who is so used to doing something one way that you avoid trying something new. The world and technology are ever-changing. If you lack the ability to adapt, your team will be affected because the team won't be able to grow. So, you want to be adaptable and fluid and be able to go with the flow and the many changes that are certain to come.

"Having poor communication skills. You want to possess excellent communication skills and be as approachable as

possible where your team is concerned. People on your team should feel like they can talk to you and not be judged. They must also feel like you value what they have to say, even if you don't agree with them.

"Don't be a know-it-all. That is definitely a bad quality to have. The smartest person doesn't know everything. Keep in mind that, as a leader, you are looking to hire your weaknesses.

"Finally, I want to give you five steps to begin building a team:

1. Write down all the necessary things you do that do not produce income.
2. Find people in your circle who you believe will add value to one another.
3. Think of income-generating ways you can actually put people in positions.
4. Find people who have a business mindset.
5. Be smart about where you are allocating money.

"Hopefully, the information I've shared will help you begin to strategically put a plan together to create the kind of team you need to get rid of those day-to-day, non-income-pro-ducing tasks. As the leader, your focus should be on the income side of your brand."

When you have an effective team working with you, it makes it easier to build your empire and leave a legacy for your family.

Millionairess Confession: *I Am a Great CEO!*

Chapter 10

Build Your Empire and Leave a Legacy

The way to build your empire and leave a legacy is by implementing the principles that have been discussed throughout this book. You do it by building relationships—wealth relationships. You do it through consistency. You do it through remaining a master student and realizing that you're going to have to keep changing. You have to keep pivoting because the world is changing, and you can't get stuck in your ways of doing things. You have to stay very teachable. Never be afraid to do the work—and know that it *will* be work. Not necessarily physical work, but it's going to be work, nonetheless.

Whether it's jumping on a Zoom call, starting on a live video, attending a conference, or even just asking a question, it's really about staying like a child—willing to learn and being teachable. Where you're just hungry to change, you're hungry to grow. And then celebrate other people's success because you cannot become anything that you're jealous of or that you hate on. Get used to celebrating people's success, and then get used to celebrating your own success. Pat yourself on the back. Be like, "Oh my gosh, I did so good." Then talk to your children about what you're doing, why you're doing it, why it's important, and why you want them to pay attention here. Why do you want them to take a look at this and talk to them about that? If you don't explain your approach, they just see your success but have no idea what the process is.

There are statistics that show that most people are not able to carry on the legacy that their parents started. That's jacked up because if the parents aren't spending enough time talking to the children about what they did and why they did it, then the kids don't know how to continue. They don't have the knowledge to know how to negotiate with the IRS because you never told them what you went through there. You never told them, "I do business with this person. I trust them here, but I would never trust them here." That information is crucial. There are people I do business with who I trust in their fields, but it doesn't mean I trust them with every area of my life. And then there may be people who I'm like, yeah, I do trust them in every area.

You've got to know the temperaments of people. You've got to know that this person's going to get it done, but better keep them behind the scenes because they don't work well with people. Or, this person is amazing with people, so you just bring them out front. All that stuff is important. I know people who are very skilled at what they do. The girl who runs my brand now, she was amazing with operations and systems, but I could not put her in front of people because she was mean. We had to work on it for a couple years, and now she's a lot better. She's a ton better, actually, but I'm still mindful to only put her in certain situations. That's all a part of building your legacy. It's not just, "This is the account number," or "This is how much is in the account." Doing business is about the processes and the relationships. It's all of that.

So again, if you're leaving a legacy, talk to your predecessors about who they can trust. Talk to them about the process. Talk to them about the failures, the challenges, the pivots. Having those conversations with them is really rewarding because otherwise, they have no knowledge. If they think that it was easy for you—not that you have to complain—but if they think it was too easy for you, then they may not be able to duplicate it. When they run into challenges, they'll quit. They're like, "Mom and Dad didn't run into them challenges." Oh yeah, we did. We sure did. We just didn't talk to you about it enough.

So the legacy has to be the success part, but it also has to be about who I can trust. Who I can trust in one part of my life doesn't mean I can trust them with every part of my life. Who works well with people, who doesn't. Bringing your family along on the journey allows them to experience or vicariously live through the failures and the successes. You want them to understand all of that. You want them in on the good, the bad—all of that. You don't want them just to know all the amazing parts.

And then we're going to go on vacation, and we're going to ball out, or we're going to shop until we drop, and we're going to go horseback riding, and we're going to do all these amazing things. So you'll get the benefits side, but also, you'll know the grit and the grind that it takes.

Jewel's Gem

Bringing your family along on the journey allows them to experience the failures and the successes.

As I've iterated countless times throughout this book, you've got to be willing to forever stay a student. You have to remain teachable and be willing to learn. Also, know that nothing is going to stay the same. So, what will build wealth today may not necessarily build wealth tomorrow. For example, I believe our grandparents—if they had enough mutual funds and CDs—probably could have become millionaires. And there are books out there, like *The Automatic Millionaire*, which I think is a great book. But it's more for a twenty-year plan, while I'm interested in quicker results than that.

This is why you have to know your advisors. I totally love and respect Dave Ramsey—he is extremely successful. But he speaks more to the average man about "get out of debt, and live below your means." And I'm not really interested in people living below their means. Still, he's an amazing financial coach, and I've learned from his teachings. But he focuses more heavily on budgeting. Now, are budgets important? Absolutely. But I really want people to get to a point where they don't sacrifice the Starbucks or sacrifice nails or hair. 'Cause I feel like that's such a big part of how you feel about yourself. So if you stop getting your nails and hair done, that's going to impact your confidence, which is going to impact your level of productivity. So I'm not interested in that path, but there's nothing wrong with what he teaches for the average guy. But for the millionairess-in-the-making, for the person who wants to be wealthy, your whole goal can't be centered around debt.

Do you need to get out of bad debt? Yes. But that can't be the whole goal. The whole goal has to be, *Let me increase my income so that I can increase the amount that I invest.* That really is where the goal needs to be. The whole goal has to be, *Increase my income so I can increase my investments, so that eventually, I can live off of the interest.* That's really where the goal needs to be.

It's also important to look at debt differently. If that debt is going to create income for you, that would be considered good debt. Also, it's important to build your personal and business credit. Personal credit—so the things like homeowners insurance, car insurance, life insurance—doesn't have crazy interests added, which increases your payments. Business credit, so that you can begin to buy assets and businesses that are in your business name, protect you from personal liability.

Again, talk to your children and family along the way, not just about the success, but the challenges: why you move in the way you move, why you had that accountant for twenty years, or why didn't you have to change that account at all. They need to see the great times, and then they also need to see how you handle pressure and conflict. They need to know why you didn't stay in business with this person. All those things are really important because if you just show them the good, it'll make them weak, and they won't know how to handle real life stuff. That was definitely the lesson that I had to learn—sharing my entire experience with my family. We would just be like, "We want to shield them from this drama or that," but drama is a part of life. It's on the inside of everybody. In the end, it was a crazy mindset to say, "I don't want them to see drama," when drama is a constant part of life.

However, in spite of the drama, sometimes you have to keep planning those family vacations where you spend time having fun and discussing goals, dreams, and desires and then planning time for yourself. Going to the spa once a month is important—that way, you'll be able to handle stress as it comes. As I said in Chapter 4, I particularly like facials and massages. For example, once I was traveling—Orlando and Houston. I was taking care of business. Then I planned my husband's birthday dinner in the same week. There were long days. Most days were probably about twelve-hour workdays. We got back from church on Sunday. Then, after church, we had some time to rest.

So, what I did is, I have two-hour massages planned—sometimes weekly, sometimes biweekly—and my massage therapist comes over and sets up in my office. I usually do it at seven o'clock at night. And that's really important for me because in any given day, a successful person may handle phone calls, conflict resolution, planning meetings, and much more. Because I'm a co-pastor of a church, a businesswoman, and a mom, I might have to handle issues in all of those roles. It may not be any bad issues—but still, sometimes I just have to be attentive to some of those things. And so you want to keep yourself in a good, healthy space physically and emotionally so that as those things come, you can handle them, and they don't knock you out.

Jewel's Gem

Going to the spa once a month is important.

Sometimes people don't grow—not because they don't want to—but because mentally and emotionally, they're just not strong enough to handle stuff. When you're feeling your weakest, millionairess, that self-care is going to be important. Also, have a good church home, stay connected, and read your Word every day. You're going to need that for your sanity. There are going to be times when you run up on some real issues and real problems, and everything can't be, and you'll think, "I'm done. I quit." Some of that stuff, you need to work through it, even though it's hard.

Even though you don't like it. Work through it. That way, you become a problem solver, and you can grow.

Jewel's Gem

Sometimes people don't grow—not because they don't want to—but because mentally and emotionally, they're not strong enough to handle stuff.

The bottom line is, if everything is, "I quit, I'm done," you don't get very far in life. You'll always be working for somebody else because people who are business owners, those people have learned how to solve problems—not just their problems, but the city's problems and even the world's problems, if you will. This is why it's so important to be emotionally intelligent and also socially intelligent. You have to spend time learning people and learning their personalities and then adding value to people. That's probably one of the biggest things a person can do: learn how to add value to people and appreciate them because when you have good relationships, you want to nurture them so you can keep them.

If you don't know how to treat people, eventually, they'll leave your life. You're like, "Lord, I need a good team," but you don't know how to treat people. You don't communicate well. You don't say "thank you." Remember that nobody really owes you anything. I know a lot of people who have not been asked back to particular tables just because their attitude was too jacked up.

Millionairess Confession: *I Am a MILLIONAIRESS!*

Conclusion

One of the first things I tell people who desire to build wealth is, you have to make a decision. And once the decision is made, you have to stick to it. Regardless of the negativity of others or your own doubts that tend to flood your mind, stick to it. When you believe God has put something in your heart and you make the decision to bring it to pass, there's no turning back. You may have to fight to stick with your decision, simply because there are seasons and times in all of our lives when we have to fight for what we want.

I believe that any woman who is willing to stick to it can become a modern-day Esther, Ruth, or Deborah. Like these women, we have not been called by God to blend in. God did not call us to be mediocre or average. We have a call and a mandate on our lives for greatness and success.

The women who join The Millionairess Club do so because they want to stretch, expand, and grow. They don't want to remain comfortable, and they no longer want to be mediocre or average. They are simply ready for more.

They also join because they understand the importance of putting themselves in positions where they are constantly given information and resources and are challenged to go to the next level. As I stated in the introduction, I believe the only difference between the rich and the poor is information. That is why I am committed to hosting my Millionairess Conferences. I want women to get hungry for the information, so their families won't ever have to live in poverty again.

Furthermore, I want to create thousands of cash and asset millionaires through my Millionairess Club. I want every woman, whether married or single, to be independently wealthy. I love to see woman who have their own money. I think it is important and empowering to be able to make decisions to do things that are important to you without needing anyone's financial assistance.

I'm Trippin'

Last year, I decided to take my daughter Cy to Italy. Of course, I checked in with my husband out of respect for him and so we could check our schedules. However, I didn't have to check in with him regarding the cost of the trip because I was able to spend my own money. It's a good feeling, and I want every woman to experience that feeling. It is so incredibly empowering to have your own money and to be able to make your own financial decisions on a daily basis.

Our trip to Italy was amazing. Cy and I both had a great time creating memories that will last forever. I remember her saying to me, "I wasn't expecting all of this." As a mom, it really felt good, being able to do that for my daughter. And I want other mothers to be in a position to plan amazing getaways with their children.

Starting out on this journey may feel a little uncomfortable at first, but that's okay. To realize your dreams, goals, and aspirations, you must get out of your comfort zone. It also requires action. You have to do more than just pray about it. Now, prayer is great because it brings revelation. However, at some point, you have to make the decision to act.

Everything you do to be successful is going to cost you something. For example, I do live webinar chats every Sunday with the members of The Millionairess Club. Although I love doing the chats, it still takes a certain amount of diligence and discipline to do it on Sundays. The other six days of the week are very busy with a few breaks every now and then. And my husband and I try to keep Thursdays open for our date night. So that leaves Sunday, which is our family day and my only day to get some rest. However, Sunday is also the day that works best for our weekly webinar chats. These chats are important to me, so I have come to terms with the fact that everything good that I desire in life is going to cost me something.

Jewel's Gem

Everything you do to be successful is going to cost you something.

I'm sure by this point in the book, your wheels are turning. Hopefully, you'll jot down a couple action steps because at the end of the day, we're definitely in an information junkie era. That can be great on one end because it's an opportunity to self-educate and to grow like we've not seen in prior years; however, we also have to be careful to make sure we don't feel pressured to do everything that we learn about. I'm sure there are a few key things that you need to hone in on, but don't let this overwhelm you. I've learned that sometimes, there are goals that God will place on my heart to accomplish for this year, but other things will be very much progressive, and it may be a two or three-year journey. Just know that if you practice learning a little bit every day, even if it's just fifteen or thirty minutes a day, then you're eventually going to meet your goals.

There are a couple of key things I want you to remember. The first being, you're not called to mediocrity—you're not called to be average. So how you move and how your schedule will look will probably not look like the girl next door—unless the girl next door is a boss, too. Secondly, remember to talk to your spouse—your boo—and your children about your vision, your goals, and your desires. Be sure to include them. Include them in the victories, and include them in the challenges and failures. Trust me, them knowing both is critical to them developing appreciation and developing good character. If all they see are wins, they'll believe that their own successes may be unachievable and that you are some phenomenon. And as you and I know, that's not true.

JEWEL'S JUMPSTART
· Set up an appointment with your banker
· Open a basic savings account
· Open up a business checking account
· Inform your banker that there may be large financial transactions on the account

Setting up an appointment with your banker is important for many reasons. It's always good to have a really great relationship with the bank, especially when the numbers start to come through so they're not constantly holding up your transactions. And then, as much as I want you to invest, you still need to have a basic savings account so that you can always have liquidity.

Remember how I talked about the importance of paying yourself? Well, if you start doing that in gold, silver, or cash, you're going to have money. So make sure that you purchase yourself a safe. I want every millionairess to have a safe in her home where she can keep cash on hand. Be sure to pick up your safe now because your days of not having any money are over. Remember, you can start small by putting $20 a week in your safe—even $10 a week. I don't care. It's the principle more than anything. You can also put your gold and silver in there, or you can choose to put it in a bank in a safety deposit box.

Time to Upgrade

I do want you to be wise in your spending. But as you're personally developing and growing, I want you to show your success externally as well. This is where you may have to get a girlfriend who has a good fashion sense. Have her give her honest opinion on your wardrobe and hairstyle. Now, listen…don't let this give you anxiety or make you feel overwhelmed. Everybody needs to start somewhere. And sometimes, you may have a look that is outdated by ten years. At one point, you may have been overweight, so all your clothes fit bigger. Girl, you just need to have a good girlfriend with some fashion sense to help you out. And again, you don't have to overspend by getting designer clothes.

There are some great consignment shops out there that you can go to and update your look. Even if you feel that you're fine in that area, double-check. Always double-check with somebody who's got good fashion sense. Clothes that you don't wear need to be given away. Having an environment that inspires you and is clean and organized is so important. I don't care if you're in a trailer right now—if you start operating an organization and prioritizing this, I promise you, it's going to clear potential cobwebs out of your head and get you on a clear path.

My mom taught me a long time ago to clean as you go. After you eat, nobody should know you were there. You should also go through your home. It might be time to upgrade your bed sheets, towels, and washcloths—some may need to be thrown out.

Lastly, when you come out of your bedroom, take the rollers out, and put on something a little cute—no wearing your night clothes around the house. Start practicing your A game privately, so having your A game publicly won't be a chore.

Are You Taking Care of You?

Since you are your brand, you have to make sure that you are taking care of yourself—in every area of your life. For instance, make sure you are booking your appointments to go see your medical doctor, the dentist, and your OB. As for the dentist, you should really be hitting them up twice a year. Bad dental health can cause bad heart health. Schedule out getting your teeth cleaned. And if you need fillings or work done, make yourself a priority and do it. In today's times, more than ever, your immune system needs to be all the way lit.

Of course, your medical doctor and your OB are annual visits, and the dentist should be a biannual situation.

The next level of self-care that I recommend is getting a membership at a spa like Hand and Stone, where you pay a monthly membership and then go every month and get massages and facials. Yes, friends, I do work on average anywhere between ten to fifteen hours a day. But you better believe my self-care is on point—including two-hour deep tissue massages bimonthly and facials sometimes once or twice a month. I play no games about how I feel or about my appearance. There's no logic in doing all of this and having you look and feel like a nightmare.

Girl Time

Definitely don't forget to get your girlfriend time in there—where you can relax, talk junk, share vision, and just have good fun. Ideally, I want you to get to a point where you're loving your life, loving what you do and the results of it, so you're not constantly looking to take breaks. Your life could be one big vacation—though I don't mean vacation in the sense of not working. I mean vacation in the sense of being fulfilled and loving what you do.

You work hard, so every now and then, you should let your hair down, go on a trip with your girls, and enjoy the fruit of your labor. This is important because it allows you to unplug, refocus, wind down, and be refreshed and ready to do life again—but perhaps with a renewed perspective.

Valued People Add Value

Always aim to add value to people who you're around, and ask God to send you the dream team. You're definitely going to need people smarter than you and people who can remind you of your goals and visions. Even though you're writing them down—hopefully every day by now—things can still fall through the cracks. No one man—or millionairess—can do everything. Have someone on your team who's good at marketing, not to mention a good IT person who can keep you up with the latest in technology and advancements to your business. You have to keep scaling—that's key.

No one wants to work with someone with a bad attitude. So, make sure being nice is your strongest attribute.

Sharing is Caring

As you make millionairess moves, don't forget to explain to your children why you made those moves. So, for example, I had a six-figure annuity that had been sitting—and I'm sure it probably had stocks in there—seven or eight years ago. So, the growth is so slow that I knew it was going to be a tax penalty if I pulled it out. But I decided to eat the tax penalty because I can take that same six-figures and quadruple it or multiply it by ten in a year's time.

Talking to your children and your network about those kinds of moves helps. It helps them to understand when they come into money and as they grow money. They'll know that just because you started something ten years ago doesn't mean that you should stay with it.

New Rules, New Tools

I know tons of people who really would be better off not investing in a 401k because the growth is way too slow. You'd be better off putting your money into disruptive innovations, like Tesla or Silicon Valley or an iRobot. You'd do better putting your money in those types of things, which have some growth.

There used to be a time where, if something had not been around for twenty, thirty, or forty years, you wouldn't trust it. Now, it's the exact opposite. You want to look for young industries that are explosive like cryptocurrency. When it comes to investing, "old" does not necessarily mean it is sustainable or even that it has longevity.

You always want to invest in areas that solve problems for people and make things easier for them. One of the reasons that Redbox took off was because they planted them in spaces all over cities where people can just drive up, like at the local Walgreens. So now, when you run into Walgreens, you can grab your Redbox too, right? It was good for a season, but as you can see, Redbox is pretty much tanked because of streaming services like Netflix and Hulu. So when you look at this particular product or this particular service and analyze it as a potential investment, always ask yourself: How will this serve humanity? Are they ahead of their time or are they on their way out?

Ideally, it's beneficial to know who's on the board and who the leaders of this company are. It will help you to be able to tell if the people in power are thought leaders; if so, regardless of how old they are, the company will probably continue to grow and expand.

If they're not thought leaders and they're fixed in the way that they operate, then more than likely, I wouldn't invest in that company. You have to make sure that when you look at investing, you look at a company's ability to change. Change is inevitable, and the faster companies change, the more likely they are to be in existence in five, ten, fifteen, twenty, possibly even fifty years. The companies that are slow to change—like that classic mom and pop shop—don't like disruption and don't like change. More than likely, those same companies will be obsolete or antiquated within the next few years.

It's important to know the technology and the thought processes of a company in order to determine whether or not this is going to be a good investment. I'm not saying that you shouldn't still have some baseline conventional products in your portfolio. But even your baseline foundational products should still have a level of moderate to fast growth potential. Otherwise, growing your wealth is probably going to be something that may or may not ever happen.

So I always look for growth potential. Traditional growth was 3 to 8 percent a year, which some would say is good. Now, if something can't grow an average of 1 to 3 percent conservatively per month, then I'm probably not going to do it. There are too many products to choose from that can really, really grow your money aggressively.

Giving Back

I started the Jewel Tankard Foundation several years ago because I wanted to make sure, as I was growing, that my giveback was just as strong. Not just giving in tithe and offering, which is definitely a priority, but giving something personal and fulfilling. Giving cars to single parents has always stuck out to me. I've given away several cars over the years, but I want to continue to increase that number. My next giveback goal is to give someone a house. I want to make sure that my growth and the expansion of my empire includes expanding investments, education, my tithe and offering, and just overall charity.

As I'm adding to my life and educating myself, I'm always pondering—how am I adding value to communities? How am I adding value to the people that I love? I want to make sure that I'm always adding value to the people around me. When you make that a priority, God finds a way to make sure that your vision and your dream is a priority because you're not just thinking about Him. You're thinking about the example of Jesus. He was a perfect example of being a giver. Everywhere He went, He was adding value to people's lives. So that's really important to me, and it's important to my team. We're always looking for opportunities to offer significant giveback.

I want to encourage you to kind of do the same thing—at your own level. Sometimes, we wait to make giving a priority until after we've made our first million or second million or whatever. But you literally could be making $40,000 a year right now and say, "This year, I'm going to give away one hundred dollars' worth of toys to a family." That's going to change a life or multiple lives. And that's really what it's all about. So, make sure you put yourself in a position where you can change somebody's life. Not just through your words but also as a demonstration of what you're able to do for them. Giving can be a family affair, a team affair, and a church affair. Everyone closely connected to you can get involved in that giveback. It's pretty amazing.

Jewel's Gem

Put yourself in a position where you can change somebody's life.

I thank you for taking the time to read my book. I hope it added some value to your life. And I want to encourage you to maybe even start a book club with this book or start reading it with your family. Hopefully, you took good notes along the way. Know that you may not implement everything that was shared, but whatever those key points are that stood out for you, I want to encourage you to share the information.

Remember that it's not just an event. Developing, growing, and expanding your empire is a journey. Stay hungry to learn. Always ask questions, and don't be afraid to try new things. You never know—it could be that new thing that totally changes everything for your family.

Now, if you are ready to step out and do what God has called you to do, I encourage you to go for it. Don't let anyone or anything stop you—not even fear. In the words of Joyce Meyer, "Just do it afraid." And while you're doing it afraid, you will also develop boldness. You see, boldness doesn't just show up. It's not like, "Oh, Lord, make me bold right now." Yes, we can pray that prayer, but boldness comes when you step out by faith, not knowing exactly where you're going or what you're doing. As a result, you develop boldness to implement whatever it is you are trying to accomplish.

I pray you are encouraged and inspired by what you have read in this book. It is God's desire for you to live a good, successful, and prosperous life. He wants to give you the desires of your heart. So, believe in yourself, and go for it. Start by connecting with people or organizations that provide financial education and resources, which will assist you in achieving the financial freedom you desire.

Now, I declare, in the name of Jesus, that you are strong, empowered, energetic, and excited about the great future God has planned for you. It's a good plan, and it is definitely a million-airess's plan.

God's Word is true. Jeremiah 29:11 says, "'For I know the plans I have for you,' says the Lord. 'They are plans for good and not for disaster, to give you a future and a hope.'" Find strength and encouragement in these words, knowing that with Him, you can and will be successful. With Him, you win.

Millionairess Confessions

1. Jesus is the Author and the Finisher of my faith.
2. I'm a generous giver and therefore, a generous receiver.
3. I give compliments daily.
4. I possess the fruit of the spirit—loving, kind, and respectful.
5. I am a winner, not a loser.
6. I win big in everything that I do.
7. I will not allow others to control my emotions negatively.
8. I allow the Word to define me, not the world. I am secure in my identity.
9. I am an anointed wife, mother, sister, friend, and teacher.
10. I influence my husband, children, family, and friends to move toward greatness.
11. I am beautiful, smart, kind, and confident in who I am and where I'm going.
12. I possess the spirit of success.
13. I am emotionally, mentally, and physically strong.
14. I dominate every situation and circumstance that I face.
15. I am financially intelligent. I will continue to expand my circle of influence.
16. I always pay my tithe and offering first and myself second.
17. I am a generous giver.
18. I am a money magnet.

19. I am out of debt.
20. My needs are met, and I have plenty more to put in store.
21. Every year, my net worth increases by 100 percent.
22. I have mentors for every area in my life, which affects my success.
23. People love me and go out of their way to help me and bless me.
24. I surround myself with people of like mind.
25. I am a millionairess.
26. Being wealthy is enjoyable.
27. When I'm in people's presences, I add value to their lives.
28. I'm extremely wealthy, and I'm extremely calm.
29. I'm a wise steward with my wealth.
30. Old and new money come to me every day and in every way, from multiple sources, easily and effortlessly.
31. I take good care of myself, my family, and those around me.
32. I have a very strong financial team that helps me to watch over and grow my wealth (for example, an accountant, tax accountant, tax attorney, and bookkeeper).
33. I love God. I love people. I love myself.
34. I am selfless and very considerate.
35. I have income-producing activity every day.
36. I partner with people who are smarter than me and have my answer.
37. I'm extremely wealthy and extremely kind.
38. I experience favor and open doors of opportunity every-where I go.
39. I am blessed to be a blessing.
40. Wealth is attracted to me.

About the Author

Author Photo: Kevin Goolsby

Jewel Tankard, economist turned financial powerhouse, is taking the world by storm. As a serial network marketer, she has grossed over $5 million and empowered over 250,000 people in her robust organizations. She has a global reputation for creating multiple six-to seven-figure earners with her success strategies.

Committed to helping women create wealth, Jewel created The Millionairess Club with over 400 members across ten countries. The club empowers women to trust their financial gut, improves their confidence, gives them cash creation and wealth-growing strategies, and introduces them to modern investment tools.

Known as the matriarch of Bravo's hit reality show *Thicker Than Water: The Tankards*, and a current star of Fox Soul's *Chatter*, Jewel is a superstar in both the business and entertainment industries. The wife of gospel jazz legend Ben Tankard, Jewel co-pastors The Destiny Center in Murfreesboro, TN, and has five children.

Be sure to visit my website and subscribe so that you can keep up with new trends concerning money. Also, you will be able to check out a lot of the resources mentioned in this book:

www.jeweltankard.com